Countryside Leisure

Terrace of three abandoned cottages in central Wales. Built of local slate stone, each is divided into two small rooms measuring approximately 10 feet by 12 feet each with fireplaces in the gable end and in the massive double chimney breasts which divide one cottage from the next. The walls are over two feet thick.

TRADITIONAL BUILDINGS
~ACCESSIBLE TO THE PUBLIC

J.R. Armstrong

EP PUBLISHING LIMITED

Acknowledgements

For the illustrations I am particularly indebted to the Weald and Downland Open Air Museum for the use of photographs and drawings which now form part of its Reference Library and Archives collection. Individual photographs were also kindly supplied by the following: the Cregneash Open Air Museum; the Stowmarket Open Air Museum; the Chiltern Open Air Museum; the National Buildings Record; Dr Brunskill, David Martin and Frank Gregory. Most of the other photographs are my own, and I am greatly indebted to Michael Coviello (Dayco Photographics) who has often improved the quality of my negatives by his skill. The cover photograph shows the Bayleaf farmhouse at the Weald and Downland Museum.

Many thanks are due to Mrs Bright and David Martin, the former for the drawings of the medieval shop at Horsham and the Wealden house at Steyning, the latter for the reconstruction of the late medieval terrace at Battle. Thanks are also due to Chris Beever who drew the maps and prepared the layout.

All the drawings, with the exception of those mentioned above, are the work of Richard Harris, and I cannot praise too highly his beautifully detailed and exact draughtsmanship which gives qualities to the book which it would otherwise lack. I am also grateful for his criticisms, realising how unacceptable he may find some of the generalisations and simplifications which I find inevitable in such a very condensed text.

Finally, I would like to thank members of the Vernacular Architecture Group who were kind enough to supply me with information which has been included in the Gazetteer. While every attempt has been made to make the Gazetteer as complete as possible there will inevitably be omissions, for which I must apologise.

About the Author

J.R. Armstrong, M.B.E., M.A. was for many years senior lecturer in social history and local studies at Southampton University. He is the author of various articles as well as *A History of Sussex* and *Local Studies*. He was the founder of the Weald and Downland Open Air Museum at Singleton in Sussex, and is now the Museum's honorary research director.

ISBN 0 7158 0678 5

Published by EP Publishing Ltd., East Ardsley, Wakefield, West Yorkshire, 1979

Photoset, printed and bound
in Great Britain by
REDWOOD BURN LIMITED
Trowbridge & Esher

Contents

To Lyn without whose encouragement and help this book would not
have been written.

Introduction

When it was first suggested that I might write a book in the 'Countryside Leisure' series suitable as a general background guide for those interested in traditional building, I considered that the only excuse for adding to the growing number of books dealing with one or other aspects of the subject would be to illustrate it throughout with examples accessible to the public, examples in which the original plan and not merely the external appearance was preserved, and, wherever possible, furnished appropriately. This was, perhaps, hoping for too much. When I began to make lists of such buildings I soon realised that there were far fewer than I had supposed. I also found that whole categories needed to be ruled out. For instance, the owners of many buildings of great interest and admirably fitted to illustrate the main theme of this book, have, in the last twenty years, received substantial grants from the Historic Buildings Council on condition that significant parts of the structure or plan should be opened to the general public on certain days of each year, or by direct arrangement by those interested. After visiting a number of such houses in which I received every courtesy and welcome from the owners it became clear that any additional publicity other than the official lists issued annually by the Council would be doing them a great disservice.

Another large class of buildings such as inns and shops had to be excluded, partly for this reason, but also because alterations and adaptations for use have usually so changed the interiors that they have become misleading. In addition, the most interesting parts of such buildings are almost invariably concealed or inaccessible. Too often also this was the case with buildings which had been converted to house a local museum, or serve some other public purpose such as a library or parish room. One also had to resist the strong temptation to go beyond the strict definition of traditional buildings adopted in this book. Most of the buildings owned by the National Trust, and the majority of those which have been adapted as museums, lie well outside its scope and purpose. To have included well-known houses such as Paycocke's in Essex, the Reader's House in Ludlow, or Churche's mansion in Cheshire and many others of similar size and status would have widened the scope and doubled its size. Because of limitations of space, the line has perhaps been drawn rather rigidly on the side of the smaller, less spectacular buildings, which give character to the local scene but which are usually neglected in favour of their more ostentatious neighbours. There are, however, some exceptions. A few of the great barns which were attached to large monastic estates or manors have been included because these buildings reveal so magnificently the structures and variations in technique and style, and some simpler communal buildings such as court rooms and market halls for the same reasons – accessibility and clarity of structure.

Finally – and this was perhaps the most discouraging fact – I found that it could be misleading to cite any buildings which I had not been able to visit in order to verify their authenticity, accessibility, and to see to what extent they illustrated the points I was trying to make. This last realisation has involved much time and travel, but as a result nearly every building referred to in the text or illustrated has been visited. Inevitably, however, there will be omissions.

On the positive side it has been heartening to find that in recent years more concern and more resources are being directed to restoration and conservation. This has followed tardily the wave of needless destruction in the name of re-development – or more often through sheer ignorance – during the two decades after the war. There are now many more of our simpler traditional buildings open to visitors. Ten years ago this book could not have been written, as nearly half the buildings which are referred to were either derelict or unrecognised for what they are, and were privately owned or occupied. The biggest contribution has

come from the creation of 'Open Air' or 'Buildings' museums. Only St Fagan's, at Cardiff, and a small museum at Cregneash in the Isle of Man have been open for more than twelve years: today every major region except the South-West has one such museum, and several have more than one. Their main concern so far has been to salvage by removal, repair and re-erection on a museum site, representative buildings which otherwise would have been bulldozed. Although re-erection on a new site is better than total destruction, it can only be second-best to preservation on the site for which the building was designed. On the other hand it does enable buildings to be restored as originally built, and their accessibility should lead to a greater realisation and appreciation of the exceptionally rich heritage of small-scale traditional buildings this country possesses, and to greater public interest in its conservation. Although these museums are in the early stages of development, they have provided the principal source of illustrative material, and in another

Part of the Open Air Museum at Hutton-le-Hole (North Yorkshire). This museum is reconstructing traditional buildings typical of one valley – Ryedale – in the Yorkshire moors. At present there are eight buildings, three of cruck construction, one of which can be seen in the foreground on the left.

Part of the Open Air Museum at Auchindrain in the South-West Highlands. This consists entirely of in-situ reconstructions of a crofters' settlement abandoned at the beginning of this century. Altogether fourteen buildings are being rebuilt and appropriately furnished. None of the buildings is probably more than two centuries old. The reconstructions will be as close as possible to the form the buildings had when they were abandoned, including repairs and patchings with alien material, but the basic structures are entirely traditional.

Group of buildings at the Weald and Downland Museum. This museum aims to represent the principal types of buildings and construction traditional in the area which the museum serves. The group illustrated will form part of a village or small town market square. Only buildings which cannot be preserved in situ are accepted. On the left is a late sixteenth-century market hall, and on the right a building entirely of brick of the early seventeenth century.

ten years probably such a book could be written entirely round these new ventures, for several more open-air museums are now being planned.

It is also heartening to find that the Department for the Environment is now more involved than used to be the case with the restoration and care of these smaller buildings. Up to a few years ago the Ministry of Works, as it was then called, was almost exclusively preoccupied with prehistoric remains, archaeological sites, castles and ecclesiastical ruins. Its very recent incursion into this neglected field includes Kirkham House at Paignton and the Black House at Arnol in Lewis (Hebrides), the latter illustrated on page 140. There are a number which cannot be included because the dates when they will be ready to open to the public are still uncertain.

'Tradition' as Interpreted in this Book

This book, then, is about traditional building – it deals with the smaller houses, farmsteads, and cottages in which the majority of the population has always lived. These buildings were the work of craftsmen using local materials – timber where timber was plentiful, stone where stone was more readily obtainable and later on brick in those areas where there were suitable clays for brick-making. The plan and layout of houses and farmsteads were slowly evolved to meet the differences of climate and occupation. Within these limits the creative imagination and technical skills of the individual were free to develop such variety of structure, plan and decoration as he felt to be appropriate. But however strong his attachment to what had been tried and proved in the past other influences have always been present – particularly that of the Church, the mansions of the aristocracy and new developments in the cities and trading centres. In the mixture which results from this interaction between the new and fashionable and the well-tried and traditional, it is not easy to draw a line beyond which the traditional has been converted into something else – élite, polite, cosmopolitan or whatever word is used to define such outside influences. Vernacular is another term used to make the distinction. Its dictionary definition is 'native or indigenous'. This puts a greater emphasis on place; which is perhaps more important than an emphasis on time or chronological continuity. But it can be very variously interpreted, ranging from the village or valley to a wider regional entity– from the individuality of a local craftsman to major schools of regional craftsmanship.

Only up to a point, therefore, can a distinction be made between traditions rooted in the locality and those adopted or imposed from outside. In the Middle Ages by far the most important external influence was the Church, and when the Gothic style was developed in the early twelfth century in a few important ecclesiastical buildings in the heart of France it had within a couple of generations affected almost every ecclesiastical building in Western Europe; but its influence did not end with the parish church. By the fourteenth century many medium-sized farm-houses in the rural areas, and small merchant's houses in the towns, would be considered out of date, or out of fashion if their doorheads were not shaped in the Gothic style. Even quite small cottages would have their main doors designed in the accepted Gothic manner. Yet the cottages themselves still remained basically traditional in plan and construction. In the same way, when the great secular buildings in the sixteenth and seventeenth centuries turned back to the classical forms revived by the

Adjacent houses at Culross, Fife. In these houses one notices a number of differences; an increase in the size of windows, in the height of doors and ceilings, a greater elaboration of window treatment, and a door surround in the classical manner. The house on the right might perhaps just be described as traditional and vernacular, but transitional; although sash windows were certainly a late and standardised introduction; but the house on the left would by general agreement be considered to lie quite outside any concept of traditional. Yet it uses local stone and tiles more conscientiously than the house on the right. It would be possible to illustrate by a series of photographs of actual houses the way in which one element in any tradition was replaced by something new or alien, eventually producing the kind of building we all recognise as non-traditional: but to fix the point in the series at which this occurred would certainly not be a matter of such general agreement.

These two open-arcaded market buildings stand side by side in the market-place at Witney, near Oxford. That on the left can be placed in the category 'traditional' being built of local stone and tile and in form and design belonging to a type of market or butter cross found in the South-West, with steep gables at different angles forming the central roof (Dunster and Chipping Campden are other well-known examples). Although the one on the right with a market hall or Guildhall over the arcade follows the form of other market halls in the area (Ledbury, Hereford, Leominster, Minchinhampton and Tetbury), the materials used are not the local stone, and the design, decorative detail and everything else about it belongs to the Renaissance – cosmopolitan or 'polite'.

Renaissance, it was not long before comparatively small cottages were given classical embellishments if only in the form of a pedimental doorhead to the entrance, while the rest of the building remained tied completely to long-established local usage. It is not easy to disentangle these elements and decide that one building is vernacular, but the building next to it is not. Two photographs on this page illustrate the point.

Also it should be borne in mind that change in the past has, for the most part, been slow and gradual, by small steps rather than by revolution. An attempt to illustrate this from one area, the most remote in the British Isles, is made in the last section of the book.

Origins

The first questions likely to be asked are – 'How far back do the seemingly firmly established traditions which we find in our earliest surviving houses or cottages go?' and 'Where did these originate?' The answers can only be tentative. It is generally agreed that in all but the extreme western areas of England we must begin with the Saxon colonisation; but in Wales, Scotland and the West of England we may have to look farther back. It is in these areas that we might expect to find some overlap with the account of domestic buildings by Dr Michael Swanton in another volume of this series, *Exploring Early Britain*. For example, the circular or oval forms of plan which seem to have been general in the Iron Age and to have continued throughout the Roman period,

Dry stone walls of a circular house built nearly two thousand years ago at Chysauster, Cornwall. The walls are still remarkably intact up to three to four feet above the original ground level.

Reconstruction of an Iron-Age farmstead in the Queen Elizabeth Country Park, Hampshire. It is based on evidence from a site at Potterne in Dorset, and includes not only a large circular aisled hut but the farm curtilage with a number of smaller structures such as cornstacks, storage pits, etc.

Reconstruction of a pigsty from Glamorgan in the Open Air Museum at St Fagans. The stones are set in clay mortar, the roof is constructed by gradual corbelling over with courses of flat stone, and the top covered with a large capping stone. In the Iron Age much larger houses were built by the same method.

are unknown on any of the early Saxon village sites so far excavated. Yet, in a few buildings – mainly pigsties – the form and corbelled method used in the well-built houses of an Iron-Age village such as Chysauster in Cornwall have persisted in parts of South Wales right into the nineteenth century, whilst the nearest analogue in England of their spacious timber-built circular houses are the very small and temporary huts built by nomadic charcoal-burners. It does, however, seem likely that the cruck method of timber building (see page 30) which is widespread in the North, the West and the Midlands, but unknown in the South-East should be traced back to a pre-Roman Celtic tradition. The evidence which we have so far from the excavated sites of early timber buildings consists solely of post-holes, pad-stones or trenches in the ground, and these are not enough to establish clearly the method of construction, but only the general plan and dimensions.

Saxon Building

In the few abandoned Saxon village sites so far examined, evidence points to a very widespread distribution of a type of dwelling, store-house or work-shop described usually as a 'sunken hut' (German: 'Grubenhaus'). In this

Two types of Saxon hut reconstructed on the excavated Saxon village site at West Stow in Suffolk. The details of construction and the kind of roof covering are bound to be largely conjectural.

Reconstructions at the Weald and Downland Museum. In the background is a Saxon sunken hut; in the foreground can be seen another way of presenting archaeological evidence without attempting to interpret it by an actual building. The short posts mark the spacing of the post-holes and give a clear idea of the plan and dimensions. Possible interpretations are given in the form of drawings adjacent at the site. It is based on excavations at Chalton, on the Sussex–Hampshire border – a site now covered over and restored to agriculture.

simple type of building the evidence can only be interpreted in one way – that of a ridge beam supported by central posts, the rafters resting on the ridge, and the floor of the hut being between one and a half and two and a half feet below the surrounding ground level. They were usually quite small, rarely more than fifteen by ten feet in floor area, though an exceptionally large one nearly forty feet long has been found on a Saxon site at Chalton. At present there is no evidence that this type of building persisted into the Middle Ages; on the other hand evidence is also accumulating for an equally wide distribution of a type of plan which is very close to the normal open-hall plan of later centuries. In these the basic structure consists of massive posts sunk vertically into the ground providing the walls, but their height – as well as that of the roof structure – remains conjectural.

Early Medieval Sites

After the Norman conquest evidence increases with every century. Since the last world war a number of villages which were deserted before the close of the Middle Ages have been excavated; even so, evidence becomes steadily less conclusive the deeper one digs, each new building partly destroying the evidence underneath. What does seem clear is that the life of the average house becomes shorter the farther back in time one goes. Many houses must have been rebuilt within the lifetime of a couple of generations and with ground plans and orientation often altered.

With the fourteenth century, in the South-East – later if we move farther west and north – our understanding both of houses and farm buildings has increased greatly in recent years. Discoveries are continually being made of buildings relatively intact concealed in later structures or additions.

Reconstruction of a small thirteenth-century cottage at the Weald and Downland Museum, based on excavated foundations of the village of Hangleton, which was abandoned in the fourteenth century.

Below is illustrated the interior before the wattle and daub partition which divided it into two rooms was completed. The main hall or living space with a central open hearth is in the foreground; in the background is a smaller room with a large oven in the corner.

This small cottage in Lincolnshire is built mainly of cob reinforced with timber, but faced on the road side with later brickwork. It is very similar in plan and dimensions to the thirteenth-century cottage from Hangleton, but is probably some four hundred years later in date with a central chimney replacing the open hearth.

These are mostly timber buildings, and represent the more solidly built and costlier structures rather than the simpler houses of the bulk of the peasantry and village communities. Of these we really know little at present before the Tudor period – ground plans, yes, but not the details of construction or decoration.

Dating

Exact dating is important to those studying the problems and concerned with tracing the origins and direction of influences, or the ways in which varying local usages overlap or combine. Until recent years accurate dating depended on documentary evidence in the few cases where this could be found: or else on secondary evidence from the form of structure, jointing or decoration. Reliance on this secondary evidence has its dangers. It cannot give due weight to local conservatism, to the exceptional importation of ideas from a distant place or even to the occasional quirks of the individual builder deliberately reacting perhaps to the rigidities of local practice. A vicious circle can be created when a form of decoration, moulding or jointing securely dated in one building is taken as a yardstick for the dating of other buildings which then give apparent authority to further dating, thus creating a trail of accredited dates apparent rather than real.

There is now some prospect of resolving this dilemma. Since the war, as a by-product of work on atomic fission, a method of dating known as 'Carbon 14' has been developed. This can be applied on all organic matter such as bone and timber to give an approximate dating (within a range of fifty to a hundred years for the Middle Ages) of the year when the timber ceased to be part of a living organism. Only a fragment of timber from a building is needed for analysis; however, this method of dating is not only costly, but the margin of uncertainty is so great that it can do little to clarify the niceties of the kind of problem the specialist researcher is trying to solve. There is, however, another method which has been given the name 'dendrochronology' (*dendros* (Greek) – tree; *chronos* – time) which may lead to far more accurate results. It is based on the examination of tree rings. The rate of growth of a tree each year varies according to the vagaries of climate during the growing period, and these variations are preserved in the width of the annular rings. In Western Europe lack of climatic uniformity theoretically makes it possible to prepare graphs which would make correlation with timber used in buildings exact, provided the timbers have a sufficient number of rings. The difficulty is to prepare a reliable master-graph for every climatic region since, within a given area, there can be surprising seasonal differences of rainfall or temperature affecting tree growth. A good deal of work has been done in Germany and in the United States, and in this country progress has been made by research centres at Oxford and Sheffield. Timbers used for the building of the Great Hall at Westminster, built at the end of the fourteenth century, are known to have been felled in a particular area, and because of their size provide data from the beginning of the thirteenth century. Samples taken from the great Cistercian barn at Coxwell in Berkshire, which lies within this region, by correlation dates the construction of the latter to the period between 1300 and 1310. This is a date from fifty to one hundred years later than evi-

Roof of the Cistercian barn at Great Coxwell; a superb example of medieval carpentry applied to a purely functional building. The exterior is shown on page 31.

dence based on decoration such as the stone corbel heads, and the form of roof construction – jointing, and other details – had suggested. Instead of being possibly the earliest barn surviving intact in this country it is now considered that several others ante-date it.

The exact opposite has happened in the case of the two great barns at Temple Cressing in Essex. As recently as 1954 it was possible for Nikolaus Pevsner to write, in the *Essex* volume of the Penguin 'Buildings of England' series: 'The barley barn is dated by experts c.1450, the wheat barn, about 1530'. Since then both these barns on the basis of an analysis of jointing and other structural techniques have been put back into the thirteenth century and this has been corroborated by Carbon 14 tests. What is now needed is a reliable dendrochronological master-graph for that region which could fix the date more exactly. These examples illustrate the uncertainty of dating by purely stylistic evidence.

Whereas there is some hope that timber buildings will be subject to increasing accuracy in dating, this is not the case with stone buildings unless the roof structure, or other timbers used, are original, which very often they are not: also in stone buildings it is often impossible to determine to what extent a building may be a partial rebuilding, or an entire rebuilding on earlier foundations; and, in some cases, where a house or barn has been extended, to determine which part was the addition and which the original.

The chapters which follow deal as concisely as possible with the patterns of traditional building as they become more clearly established from the fourteenth century onwards. From each century the number which survives with relatively little alteration increases dramatically until, by the seventeenth and eighteenth centuries, one is dealing with hundreds of thousands of individual buildings and with whole villages which still preserve, with as yet little alien intrusion, the forms developed in the past.

The illustrations with their captions are chosen where possible to cover points additional to those brought out in the very generalised text, and, at the end of each section some guidance on further reading is given.

Recommended Further Reading

There are a number of books which are relevant to almost every chapter, and these are listed below. Others which have particular relevance to the subject of each chapter are listed at the end of the appropriate chapter.

C.F. INNOCENT, *The Development of English Building Construction.*

S.O. ADDY, *The Evolution of the English House.*

These two books were written three-quarters of a century ago and were pioneering works in the study of our traditional buildings. Both the authors were Midlanders, and it was perhaps their great knowledge of these areas that led to some over-emphasis – such as that cruck building was an almost universal form of early construction, and (by Addy in particular) the assumption that the longhouse was normal among our Anglo-Saxon forebears. Neither generalisation is factual, but both books are full of interesting material.

SALZMANN, *Building in England Down to 1540.*

A book to be particularly recommended to those interested in documentary records. It covers every aspect of early building from the prices of materials, the kind of contracts made and the status of different craft workers in the building trade, to a consideration of actual buildings and their construction.

NATHANIEL LLOYD, *History of the English House.*

A comprehensive work, but concerned more with the larger houses than with those which lie within the category of vernacular.

ERIC MERCER, *English Vernacular Houses.*

A monumental work; many of the illustrations are of buildings demolished since the war and recorded by the Royal Commission for Historic Monuments.

R.H. BRUNSKILL, *Illustrated Handbook of Vernacular Architecture.*

An extremely clear and valuable guide for those who wish to take their general interest further and continue much-needed research on the subject. It has particular relevance to the north of England which the author knows most intimately.

Apart from the books recommended, there are the very large number of detailed guides and monographs written for most of the buildings cited or illustrated. For all the material tucked away in the annual journals of various learned societies and local archaeological societies, one can refer the reader to *A Bibliography on Vernacular Architecture* published in 1972 and on the reference shelves of most public libraries.

Buildings in the Landscape

Confused areas of Limestone and Sandstones of varying quality including Millstone Grit ⊠

Carboniferous Limestone and Sandstone ▤

Areas deficient in good building Stone ▦

Greensand Belt (Limestone and Sandstone) ▥

Chalk and Flint ▦

Oolitic Limestone and Sandstone ▤

Old Red Sandstone ▨

Granite ▦

Wealden Clays and Sandstone ▨

Note: The areas left blank are areas where forms of Building Stone are so varied that detailing would be either too confusing or over simplified. This applies also to the regional maps in the Gazetteer

The geological structure of England and Wales.

Typical group of buildings below the chalk escarpment where greensand, chalk and clay strata come close together. The group includes (1) flint with an inner lining and infill of chalk in the building on the right, (2) upper and lower greensand stone in the wall and building on the left. The pegtiles, brick quoins and window edges were almost certainly made in the brick and tile works that existed up to the beginning of the present century within a mile of the site, on the gault clay beds to the south. Laminated stone tiles known as 'Horsham stone' on the roof of the farmhouse came from the Weald clay which reaches to within half a mile to the north. The brick and stone work of the farmhouse has been plastered, and the whole of the front colourwashed recently. Such a mixture of materials could only occur in the narrow belt, at the most three miles wide, which runs below and parallel with the chalk escarpments of South-East England.

All buildings of the kind we are dealing with in this book were closely knit to their environment. Up to the end of the eighteenth century, difficulty in transporting heavy materials ruled out the use of anything not locally available; and the lie of the land, contour, shelter and accessibility to a spring of running water played a vital role. It is the use of local stone, timber, clay, thatch or tile which we notice first, and it is this which relates a building more than anything else to the surrounding landscape of which it forms a part. If we look at the geological map of this country and compare it with any region of similar size in Europe we are immediately struck by the variety and rapidity of change from one geological area to another; subdivisions are usually smaller and irregularities far greater. It is this more than any other factor that has given this country a variety of local forms of building unsurpassed elsewhere. There are few counties in the British Isles without sudden and dramatic changes in the landscape and in the buildings in that landscape. These can still surprise us, even after a century and a half of steady submersion under amorphous development and the use of materials seldom related in any way to the locality.

In any study of traditional building we need, therefore, to start with some understanding of the geology and geomorphology of the district. One general division that can be made is between upland and lowland. On the whole this determines not only the materials used – stone mostly in the uplands and timber in the lowlands – but it also determines differences in farming and therefore in the layout and design of farms, in the siting and character of the village settlement, and so on. This division between upland and lowland is not, however, clear-cut, and large areas of England and parts of Wales and Scotland do not fall neatly into either category. Also, within such a classification there can be very abrupt geological transitions so that the character of buildings and settlements can change suddenly and completely within a couple of miles, and within the confines of one parish.

For example, many parishes situated under the scarp slopes of the Downs of Kent, Surrey and Sussex stretch within half a dozen miles across areas as diverse as the chalk and flint region of the Downs, through the various greensand beds (each producing totally different types of stone both in colour and in texture) to the heavily forested regions of the Weald clay. Within these parishes almost all buildings with the exception of the church, and perhaps the manor-house, were, up to the eighteenth century, built of materials im-

One end of a field barn in the Bonsall district of Derbyshire, an area where the limestone and gritstone strata of the Pennines meet. The steps, door surrounds and corners are all of squared gritstone, the main structural infill of rough, unsquared rubble limestone. This is the usual combination in the districts where these stones, very different in colour and texture, are adjacent. Farther north one moves into gritstone only.

mediately accessible, in most cases within a few hundred yards: flint and chalk on the Downs, grey limestone from the upper-greensand, brown sandstone from the lower-greensand with oak timber-framing and brick concentrated more on the clay belt. This kind of local pattern persisted up to the introduction of alien materials by canal, rail and ultimately by road, during the last two hundred years. Each new development in transport cut more and more deeply into the traditional pattern.

Sudden juxtapositions like this occur in almost every county. The dramatic transitions in parts of the Pennines between the dark, coarse millstone grit and the limestone affect not only the general character of the landscape and villages, but also details of construction such as the way stone is used in jointing and coursing, or the forms of mouldings, of window and door surrounds and roofing. Another example is the wide belt of oolitic stone which stretches diagonally across the Midlands from Stamford in the north-east to the Dorset coast in the south-west. The stone from these beds

varies greatly from the central areas of the Cotswolds with its golden-tawny colour and close texture to the greyer, rougher stone to the north and to the south. There are many places where one can see this transition between one village and the next.

There are, again, the borderline areas in which these geological divisions merge and interpenetrate. In such areas buildings reflect the geological ambiguity of their environment — often two or three types of local stone being used in one small building. It is possible in such cases to trace on the map a band, perhaps not more than two or three miles wide, following the lines of geological cleavage. Within this belt one could locate with reasonable certainty a village, or even a single building, simply by observing the range of materials used.

Lacock, Wiltshire. A village near the western edge of the oolite belt, of mixed materials typical of such border areas. Nearly half the buildings are timber-framed (an exposed cruck can be seen in the cottage wall at the end of the street). There is laminated stone tiling throughout with the exception of the building on the extreme right with its recent and quite alien pantiling.

Castle Combe, Wiltshire. A typical village within the oolite belt, built almost entirely of the local stone with rubble walls and cleft stone tiling, and with chimneys of neatly jointed trimmed stone. The stone is lighter in colour than that in the Cotswolds, farther to the north.

The nine regions into which, for convenience of reference, the Gazetteer which forms the second part of this book has been divided correspond to the principal geological divisions; but there are two exceptions. The first is the great belt of chalk and flint which passes through four regions stretch-

Granite masonry in a longhouse dating possibly from the fourteenth century, on the edge of Dartmoor. Note the exceptionally fine stone cutting and jointing and the uncoursed rough rubble above the two openings – presumably repair work of a later date.

Detail of roughly knapped and squared flint walling with flint chippings used to decorate and protect the mortar joints – a technique typical of parts of West Sussex.

Detail of very finely knapped and squared flint walling with exceptionally close jointing – a refinement perfected in East Sussex and some other areas of the South-East.

ing from Dorset in the South-West, through the Salisbury Plain into the Midlands, then branching to the South-East via the North and South Downs, and to the East and North through East Anglia and Lincolnshire, petering out eventually in the Yorkshire Wolds. Within each of these regions through which the chalk belt passes distinctive local traditions have developed in the use of flint.

Although, with the single exception of the Fenland, there is no large area without some form of usable building stone, wherever there was an adequate supply of timber the latter was used for the great majority of our smaller buildings, at least up to the seventeenth century. For the most part this coincided with the most densely populated and prosperous areas with soil suitable for agriculture as well as for a plentiful supply of oak which probably constituted three-quarters or more of the timber used in building. Oak was certainly grown in many areas of the South-East as a crop, carefully planned and cycled to supply the sizes and shapes of wood required. This was the situation over most of the country until the seventeenth century, when the growth of population and the diminution of woodland resources began seriously to affect the supply. Before that, in areas where excellent building stone was easily accessible – such as the Cotswolds or the flint areas of the chalk – a good deal of timber building is found side by side with the dominant stone or other material.

The regional styles of timber building do not relate to the landscape in quite the intimate way of local stone. Regional and local variations were quite differently determined. It is, however, possible to make generalised statements about

An assortment of decorative timber-framing in Ludlow (Shropshire). The highly ornamental central building, with its elaborately cusped panelling is typical of the West Country, but the buildings to right and left could not be so certainly 'placed'. Looking at the timber-framing of the building on the right, the awkward proportions of the top row of panelling, and the pitch of the roof indicate that the roof was raised at some time – spoiling the proportions of the original upper storey.

wide regionally distributed forms, and about the lesser variations within these regional forms, even to the differences in parishes and hamlets. Some of these are illustrated and commented on in the Gazetteer. They make an immediate visual impact which is exaggerated by the practice, relatively recent, of emphasising the timber-framing by staining it black. The fascination of timber buildings lies, perhaps, in the way it reflects the changing and precarious, but ever-present, balance between tradition or control by custom and the perpetual urge towards individual or group expression. We can trace the over-all acceptance of a regional pattern or 'vocabulary', and see how it was then possible to express some measure of local distinction or difference, and so on down to the individual builder or carpenter. In the study of timber-framing we can also find reflected strikingly the changes and differences in aesthetic values between one area and another, and between one period and another.

What is true of timber is true of another material with much less striking visual impact, namely, brick. Its adoption was late in this country. Apart from the making, and very limited use, of bricks in the Hull area, and of some imported brick (presumably brought over as ballast in ships returning from the Continent) in the coastal areas of East Anglia and in the immediate vicinity of one or two ports in Kent and Sussex, brick was neither made nor used in this country between the Roman occupation and the end of the fifteenth century. It is difficult to understand why: unless it was because of the ample supplies of timber and the great variety of excellent local stone. Just across the Channel brick had been used for castles, cathedrals and civic buildings, but in England it was not until the building of Hurstmonceaux castle in the South-East and one or two buildings such as Tattershall castle in Lincolnshire in the mid-fifteenth century that any major building in brick was constructed.

Hurstmonceaux was built by a veteran of the Hundred Years' War familiar with the great brick fortresses of north-eastern France. He imported Flemish brickmakers and bricklayers to do the work. These buildings were soon followed by a number of great and influential buildings, such as

Early seventeenth-century brickwork of a building which has now been re-erected at the Weald and Downland Museum. It illustrates the form of bonding general up to the middle of the seventeenth century – 'English bond' – where the solid walls are bonded together by laying bricks in alternate courses lengthways and endways. The original large three-light window with moulded brick mullions was infilled in the central section and a stone inserted with the date 1772 – the year when the building was repaired after a fire had gutted the interior. Date-stones can sometimes be misleading.

King's College, Cambridge and Hampton Court Palace, and it was used as a basic structural material with an exterior casing of stone for the central King Harry tower at Canterbury Cathedral. By the mid-sixteenth century brick had become almost a prestige material, as highly valued as stone, and much of the finest and most elaborate brickwork in this country was done in that period. It is true that the technique of brickmaking improved at a later date, but the quality and expressiveness in its decorative use was not surpassed. What started at the aristocratic level soon filtered down to the vernacular and was adapted to the existing tradition, quickly developing its own range of local variation. It was soon used in conjunction with stone, particularly where stone such as flint presented difficulties to the building of neat door or window frames and corners (quoins). It was also soon used as a more esteemed alternative to the traditional wattle-and-daub infill as walling material between timber framing.

Other broad regional divisions can be made in the use of materials, such as cob, which is found particularly in the South-West, but in one form or another is also used in pockets of the Midlands and East Anglia, although so far it has not been found in the extreme south-eastern counties. In each

The end of a partly collapsed cob wall (Wiltshire). Its tapering form and mixed ingredients can be seen, also the way in which cob was built up – layer by layer in three distinct horizontal divisions. Each layer needed to set hard before the next was added. Protection from rain was essential, and the collapse of this wall was clearly due to the loss of its protective capping which originally may have been stone tiles or thatch.

Early brick infill between the timber-framing of an upper-floor hall at Laxfield in Suffolk (now a local museum). The decoration on the horizontal beam of the jetty is typical of the area, and the infill attractively patterned.

area it is used in different ways. Basically it is a mixture of clay, stone and straw built up in layers in walls that taper from ground level – where they may be as much as two and a half feet thick – to the eaves, where they may be less than eighteen inches. Provided it is protected from rain by roof overhang, coping and an outer coat of water-shedding mixture such as lime combined with cow-dung, it can be as durable as any other material, with excellent insulation against heat and cold. Its quality and texture depend upon the materials to hand; in the old red sandstone region of

south-east Devon the walls have a colour which matches the reddish tinge of a freshly ploughed field; in parts of Cornwall walls are mostly rough in texture, often bulging, reflecting the quality of the broken stone of which the cob is mostly composed. In Lincolnshire and parts of East Anglia cob is combined with a rudimentary stabilising timber-frame.

Decoration of buildings is secondary to the materials used, but most decoration develops from the characteristic properties of these materials and from the structure. Any critical

This unusual photograph was taken during the demolition of a two-storey cob house in Buckinghamshire. This form of cob was known locally as wychert; a main constituent was broken fragments of hard chalk or 'clunch'. The photograph shows the chimney on the right half demolished. The material has been removed to the site of the proposed Open Air Museum for the Chiltern Area; the intention is to reconstitute the mixture and rebuild the house exactly as it was.

assessment of the quality of decoration must take into account integration or appropriateness of this kind; the variety and subtle forms developed, often by local craftsmen working within an accepted regional tradition are sometimes delightful, sometimes surprising, and always intriguing.

A rear view of the Guildford House Gallery (High Street, Guildford, Surrey). At first sight this would be taken to be a brick building. In fact, from the first floor upwards it is entirely timber-framed clad with mathematical tiling. One's suspicions might be aroused by the character of the 'brickwork' which consists entirely of headers, and the curious unevenness of the surface at the top left of the projecting oriel window.

Decoration as such is not the theme of the present chapter, but there are forms of applied decoration which can so transform the whole external appearance, concealing structure, or even creating the illusion of a different structural material, that they must be considered. This is also complicated by the fact that it is not always easy to discriminate between the cladding of walls for structural reasons (or as part of the structure) and arbitrarily applied surface decoration added at a later date. An example is the widespread use of various forms of tile-hanging on walls of timber-framed buildings (and occasionally on stone or brick buildings) particularly prevalent in the South-East in the eighteenth and nineteenth centuries. This was almost certainly first adopted to provide better protection against damp than the wattle-and-daub or brick infill in timber-framed buildings provided, or to cover soft mortar jointing and porous brick or masonry. In some areas, however — and this also applies to slate-hanging in the South-West — the purely decorative motive becomes more important and supersedes the practical purpose, the façade side being covered but not the weather side. The most striking example perhaps was the development in the South-East of what is known as 'mathematical tiling'. This simulates

Detail of a house façade in the limestone region of Derbyshire showing how the original rubble limestone wall was later covered with plaster and incised to imitate ashlar stonework. This kind of transformation can be seen in other materials — rough brickwork, for example, was sometimes covered with a reddish cement which was then pointed to simulate finest flush brickwork.

brickwork and was applied usually only to the façades of buildings. Some regional uses of other forms of wall cladding such as weather-boarding and decorative plaster (pargetting) are illustrated in the Gazetteer. One general point, however, should be made: not only can the decorative treatment of exteriors be quite unrelated to either structure or material, but it can also be changed easily and cheaply. A coat of colourwash costing a few pounds and a day's work can destroy completely the skill and good taste of a flint-knapper, stone-mason or bricklayer who may have devoted weeks to the detailing and perfection of their work.

On some of the great estates, eighteenth- and nineteenth-century landowners attempted to give a distinctive appearance to the buildings within their control, producing effects which sometimes were interesting but which were quite unrelated to the actual locality – such, for example, as the round-headed brick windows inserted into houses, schools, inns and cottages on the Dering estate, west of Canterbury. Whether the basic structures were of stone, brick or timber-framing was not taken into consideration, and the estate cuts right across natural geological and landscape divisions. The same kind of thing can develop, however, from

Leaded lights in a terrace at Rochdale.

below, and one need not go back to the last century to find the process at work. There is, for example, an area round Rochdale and Bolton where the traditional building material has for centuries been the local dark brown sandstone. Industrialisation in the last century led to rows and rows of identical terrace houses, still built in the local stone. Early in the present century some local individualist introduced patterned leaded-lights into the front door and parlour windows. Within a few decades this was adopted as an accepted local fashion. In this case we may see it as an attempt at individual expression, a protest against the uniformity and impersonality of the terraced house design. In the same way countless new estates of identical houses in the twentieth century are relieved commonly by differences in the colour of the paintwork. One needs to remember that few small cottages or houses were, until the seventeenth century, exactly alike, whereas from the middle of the eighteenth century most are identical with their immediate neighbours.

As striking in its visual impact as the materials of walls or the spacing of doors and windows, can be the roof covering

A building on the Dering estate, Kent, with inserted round-headed windows on the sides facing the road.

Heather thatching laid over a turf base at Auchindrain Open Air Museum.

of a building. This is so generally realised that a ban is placed by many local authorities on the use of certain alien materials – such as asbestos – yet there are few villages free from obtrusive Welsh slate which was introduced very widely in the late eighteenth and early nineteenth centuries. This material is inappropriate to any area outside the slate landscape from which it came, but is efficient and durable. In colour and texture it can be more disastrously inappropriate even than asbestos. We are, however, faced with a very real difficulty when dealing with roof covering. It is that part of a building which is most expendable and most subject to replacement and alteration. The impact which many villages in the South-West and parts of East Anglia make on the casual visitor is due to the amount of thatch or the particular texture of local tiling, though in many cases the original roof covering may have been quite different. There is, for example, considerable evidence from early accounts that wooden shingles of cleft oak were widely used for every type of building; as they still are over large areas of Scandinavia, Germany and Central Europe. Occasional fragments preserved in acid soil conditions have been found on various medieval sites excavated within the last few years; but later their use seems to have become gradually confined to the

steep wooden spires of churches, mostly in the South-East. It is also often assumed that thatch was almost universal on the smaller and humbler buildings. This again may be quite mistaken. Clay roofing tiles were widely used in the South and East in the thirteenth century, and fragments of ornamental finials, ridge tiles and decorative smoke outlets (louvres) are found fairly widely, and some still remain intact on the roofs of a few houses in Cambridgeshire and East Anglia. In fact, we probably tend to under-estimate the amount of purely decorative detail of this kind which was lavished on even the humblest buildings. A number of houses in a deserted medieval village site at Hangleton in Sussex had been roofed with stone tiles brought by sea from Cornwall or Devon – a striking exception from the dependence on materials immediately to hand, because easy sea transport was possible. (In the same way the occasional use of early Flemish brick is found in the South-East.) How far thatching was general in corngrowing areas where other materials were not so easily acquired and of what quality the thatching may have been, it is quite impossible to determine; but there is no reason to assume that the craftsmanship was inferior, or that the decorative element was less, than in the thatcher's craft today. In many towns there were restrictions on the use of thatch, and in some the limewashing of thatch was enforced as a safeguard against fire. There are cases where examination shows

Combed wheat straw thatching on the treadwheel house at the Weald and Downland Open Air Museum.

that cottages thatched in the nineteenth century, perhaps for reasons of economy, were, before that, tiled – a downgrading which is almost the reverse of the current trend.

The last illustration in this chapter is of the roofing of a re-erected fifteenth-century upper hall at the Weald and Downland Museum. The stone tiles are of an exceptionally thick and heavy laminated sandstone known locally as 'Horsham stone'. On large church roofs slabs of this stone can weigh a hundredweight. These large stones are set on

Solid or 'dead' thatch, still found on farm buildings in the Cotswolds. Brushwood is heaped on poles or sawn timbers laid flat from eave to eave to form a slope to the centre or 'ridge'. Straw thatch is then laid on top of this. The illustration shows thatching in progress at Cogges Manor Farm, Witney, Oxfordshire.

Heavy stone tiles being laid on a roof of the fifteenth-century jettied upper hall at the Weald and Downland Museum.

the lowest course, both the courses and the size of the stones diminish as they ascend to the ridge. This technique is almost universal where stone tiles are used, the main exception being the easily shaped though thin and hard Welsh slate. Visually, these diminishing sizes are very satisfying, but the technical skill involved is great, and the repair of such roofs costly. In few areas are these traditional forms of stone roofing still attempted, and in most areas repair consists in their entire replacement by modern cheaper and lighter materials. In some areas no quarries remain so that replacement becomes difficult or impossible. Synthetic substitutes are being made, but these are rarely quite satisfactory visually, and if, as often happens, they become used in areas where the true local materials have different qualities, either in texture or colour, they further disrupt the relationship of buildings to their natural setting.

Recommended Further Reading

ALEC CLIFTON-TAYLOR, *The Pattern of English Building*.
> This is not only the book most relevant to this chapter, but is beautifully illustrated and clearly written. The only reservation can be that it does not cover Scotland or Wales, and is more concerned with the greater buildings.

N. DAVEY, *Building Stones of England and Wales*.
> A concise little handbook plotting surviving quarrying areas and the main types of stone.

M. A. ASTON, *Stonesfield Slate* (Oxford Museum Service).
> A study in the use of Cotswold stone.

NATHANIEL LLOYD, *History of English Brickwork*.
> A pioneer work but still the most comprehensive available, and it gives some attention to smaller buildings.

A. CLIFTON-TAYLOR, *English Brickwork*.
> A more recent and more concise work than the above.

Mention should be made of the Penguin 'Buildings of England' series now completed. It has not been much concerned with the smaller traditional buildings which are the subject of this book, but the introductory reviews to each county, dealing with its geological structure and position in the general pattern of cultural influences, are invaluable.

Structure and Building Techniques

To appreciate fully any building we need to know how it is put together: just as our appreciation of decoration depends in part at least on our knowledge of the qualities of the material used. This is particularly true of building in timber; and even where either stone, cob or brick was the principal walling material, wood still played an essential part in the roof, doorways and windows.

As we have seen, the usual technique in Saxon building was to sink posts directly into the ground, usually fairly close together with no suggestion of divisions or 'bays' or more heavily built trusses. This tradition seems to have continued throughout the Middle Ages, but was by its nature short-lived so that only post-holes record its use. The other more durable forms of construction can be divided into three main categories.

The first is that in which the whole building hangs as it were on a framework of paired, curved timbers described as 'crucks' or 'cruck blades', and, when joined together, as a 'cruck truss'. These curved timbers extend from ground level to ridge; the number of pairs determined the length of the building, and the distance between one and the next is termed a 'bay'. The width and height of the building, therefore, depended entirely on the size and curvature of the crucks. The roof is mainly supported by the cruck which, resting on the ground and joined at the apex, gives complete stability to the whole roof structure, since the walls can be regarded as free-standing and only incidentally help to sup-

port the roof.

The second form is sometimes called 'post and panel', or, more often, 'box frame'. In this the main structural elements consist of uprights which, instead of being sunk in the ground, rest on massive horizontal timbers and are kept rigidly in position by being tenoned into this 'bottom plate' or 'sole plate'. These posts are connected across the building at eaves level by massive 'tie-beams' and horizontally by 'top-

Cruck barn from Herefordshire at Avoncroft Museum of Buildings, during re-erection. This illustrates clearly how the main weight of the roof is borne by the cruck, not by the walls.

28

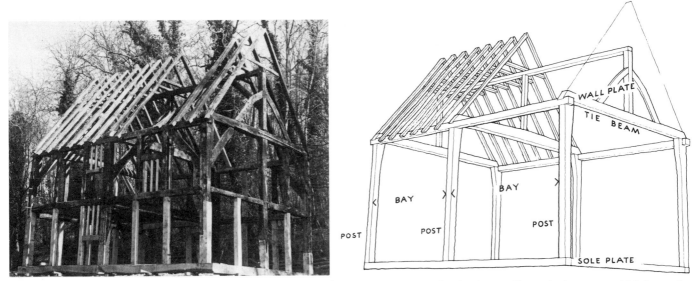

Box-frame roof of a house during re-erection at the Weald and Downland Museum. Every piece of timber is jointed by projecting tenons which fit exactly into mortices made to receive them. Holes are drilled through these joints and the joint secured by wooden pegs; but even without the pegs the structure would normally remain stable.

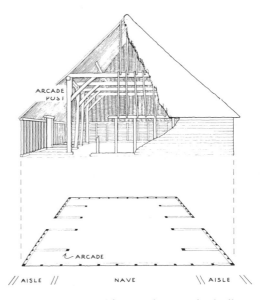

Aisled barn during re-erection at the Weald and Downland Museum. The completely independent structure of the central nave is clearly illustrated; the accompanying diagram clarifies both the plan and the structure.

plates', 'eaves plates' or 'wall plates'. The eaves plates in turn support the feet of the rafters, which may be connected to a 'ridge beam' or simply joined together in pairs at the apex.

The third form is that of a much wider roof structure, supported by intervening posts. These, when regularly placed, form a central 'nave' with 'aisles' in which the 'arcade' or 'aisle posts' support the eaves. The aisled form was the only way by which a large space could be roofed. In domestic buildings this would apply to manorial halls and the greater houses, but in a few areas it was employed in smaller houses and persisted throughout the medieval period.

In all three forms the building was divided into bays between the main supporting frames or 'trusses'. The width between one truss and the next depended partly on the size and strength of the timbers used, and partly on the needs of interior planning and proportion, such as the size of rooms, or to articulate the space within a large room such as the open hall. This division of the structure into bays and bay trusses is fundamental to the understanding of the way in which house plans developed. In cruck construction this was logical and inevitable, and it has been suggested that the articulated box-frame stems from, or at least was influenced in its development by, cruck construction.

Within these basic forms of timber construction there was a very wide range of secondary variation, particularly in the roof structure. Each variation suggested new forms of decoration and design. It is impossible to be sure where or when these different traditions started. With cruck building, for example, it was an established method of building over a wide area in the West and North of England by the thirteenth century, and as none survive which can be assigned to an earlier date it has been suggested that it might be a relatively late development by carpenters copying the Gothic arch which revolutionised masonry building in the twelfth century. There is no correlation between the spread of Gothic and the distribution of early cruck buildings. The latter is confined to the northern parts of Germany and the Netherlands, and the North and West of this country; but it can be argued that an existing tradition was given a new life by its association in style with the Gothic arch of the stone-

30

Areas where Cruck construction is dominant

Mainly jointed Crucks

Area within which Cruck construction is found

Area within which Crown Post and Collar Purlin roof construction is prevalent

Mainly jointed Crucks

The geographical spread of cruck construction.

Great Coxwell barn. The interior is shown on page 14.

masons, for there was a very close link between masons and carpenters in the Middle Ages. The mason relied on the carpenter for much essential auxiliary work – shuttering to support the ribs of arches, doors and window heads, and the carpenters copied the forms of moulding and other decoration evolved by the masons. It is therefore quite likely that an established but simple type of timber structure was given a prestige which led to its adoption in large, sophisticated and richly decorated buildings. From the pattern of its distribution it seems probable that cruck building is something

carried over from a Celtic pre-Saxon culture, but for the Saxons was a form which they neither introduced nor favoured.

Cruck Construction

The detailed study and analysis of cruck construction has really only been undertaken during the last few decades, and has led to a classification of types and more exact distribution maps. Some of the main forms are illustrated in the photographs and drawings on pages 32–3.

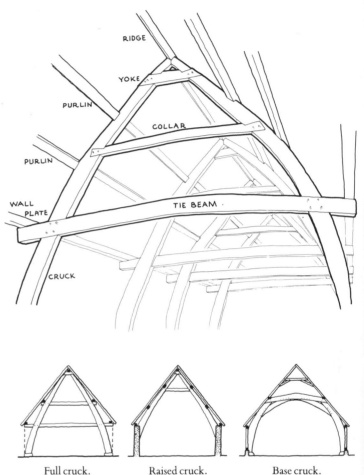

RIDGE

YOKE

PURLIN

COLLAR

PURLIN

WALL PLATE

TIE BEAM

CRUCK

Full cruck.　　Raised cruck.　　Base cruck.

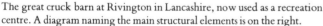

The great cruck barn at Rivington in Lancashire, now used as a recreation centre. A diagram naming the main structural elements is on the right.

A distinctive feature of all crucks is that the 'blade', as it is called, tapers towards both ends, the thickest section being that on which the greatest strain is exerted. The blades of some of the larger cruck buildings may exceed two feet in width in this part, but may be less than four inches thick. In fact crucks are used in the same way as timber is used today, in contrast to the usual medieval practice in joists and rafters of setting them flatways to the weight they carry rather than

edgeways, the loss in strength being compensated for by the excessive size of the timber used.

Crucks were created by cleaving or sawing down the middle a carefully selected naturally curving trunk or branch so that mirror-image pairs were produced, ensuring exact symmetry when placed opposite. Cleaving was also appropriate to other paired timbers such as rafters, or the pointed frames or 'durns' of medieval doors. It is also a

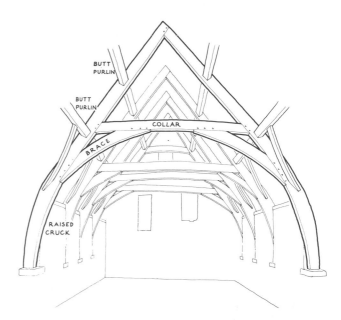

Raised cruck barn at Lacock (Wiltshire). Explanatory diagram on the right.

Rudimentary jointed-cruck of a building being re-roofed at the Auchindrain Open Air Museum near Inverary.

Looking up at the roof of the great fifteenth-century barn at Drayton St Leonards. It will be seen that many of the rafters are slightly crooked, and a few near the ridge, very crooked. This does not matter provided the cleft side, which supports the battens and tiles, lies evenly and is straight.

possible reason why medieval rafters are laid flat rather than on edge, since any slight irregularities are taken up horizontally rather than vertically.

Although full cruck structures have nowhere yet been identified in the South-East, a certain number of buildings have recently been found where a form of curved timber was used as a principal structural element. In these houses a very sharply curved timber takes the place of what would otherwise have necessitated an arcade post and an aisle. The term 'quasi-aisle' or 'quasi-cruck' has been used to describe this.

Whereas the cruck tradition was restricted to the West and to the North, the box-frame is to be found everywhere. It must have had a long period of development before the earliest surviving examples, none of which can be dated back beyond the twelfth century. The decoration of some Saxon stone churches, such as Earl Barton in Northampton-shire, suggests timber-framing, and recent archaeological evidence has revealed the existence of plates with mortices. Although most Saxon buildings seem to have been constructed of posts sunk fairly close together directly into the ground, and without bay divisions or main supporting trusses, there is sufficient evidence to suggest that there were also buildings of box-frame construction. The difficulty is that such buildings leave far less evidence in the ground — perhaps trenches, but nothing else.

Tithe barn at Bredon in Worcestershire. The great post and roof structure is simple and unornamented compared with that shown in the photograph at the foot of page 35.

Aisled Buildings

The third main structural form, the aisled, is, like all main architectural devices, derived from the problem of roofing. The simplest way of giving intermediate support to rafters is by plates supported on posts rising directly from the ground inside the building. As early as the Neolithic period large structures were built in this way, and from this form of timber building both the Roman basilica and the aisled church were descended. The largest Saxon timber buildings,

Conjectural reconstruction of aisled hall from East Kent, in store at the Weald and Downland Museum.

KING POST

Kingpost truss in the roof of the barn at East Riddlesden Hall, Keighley, W. Yorks. The kingpost rests on the middle of the tie and supports the ridge-beam. This is reminiscent of the type of early Saxon construction in which central posts rose directly from the ground to the ridge as in the sunken huts. This tie beam, kingpost and ridge structure is widespread over most of the Midlands and North.

Octagonal arcade post with moulded capital at Edgar's Farm re-erected at the Stowmarket Open Air Museum (Suffolk).

such as the Great Hall at Cheddar in Somerset, were of this form. It was employed throughout the Middle Ages in public buildings such as hospitals and guildhalls and large farm buildings such as barns. In domestic buildings, however, the aisle posts were presumably found to be an intrusion on the living space, and, except in parts of East Anglia and the Midlands, aisles are found only in the largest houses. A contributing factor may be that the aisled form in the smaller domestic buildings meant low windows which, when shuttered against wind and weather, would not only exclude wind and rain but also all light. By eliminating the aisle the height of the windows could be raised and adjustment to weather conditions made more flexible by closing only the lower part. This may explain why even small open halls had windows usually on both sides of the hall. This need for flexibility in shuttering might also explain why, in the later Middle Ages, houses with just one aisle were built. The rejection of the aisled form is illustrated by the fact that many early aisled houses seem to have had the aisles removed before the end of the Middle Ages.

Roof Structure

Secondary to these main structural forms are the variations in roof construction. The principal forms are illustrated in

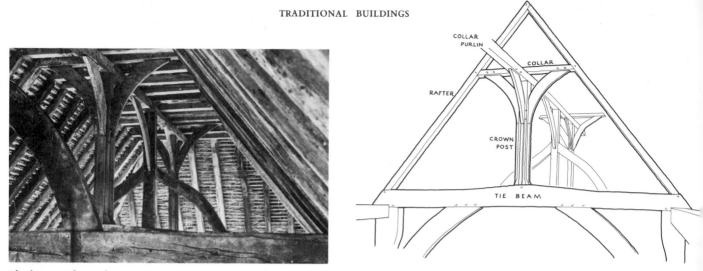

The kingpost form of construction was never developed in the south. In the thirteenth century the crownpost and collar-purlin form of construction illustrated in this photograph of Bayleaf farmhouse at the Weald and Downland Museum became general. In this form of construction the ridge-beam is dispensed with and a shorter post ('crown post') supports a longitudinal beam ('collar purlin') which in its turn gives support and stability to 'collars' which join the rafters. This ingenious and stable form of construction lent itself to considerable decorative elaboration in the larger buildings.

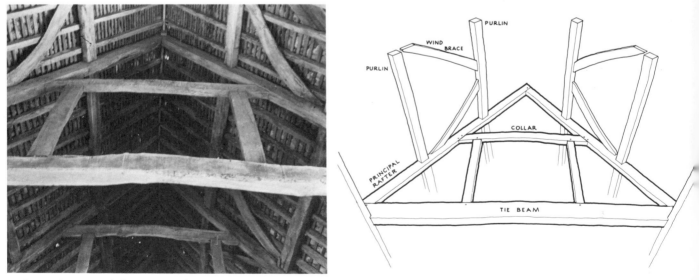

In the South-West and the West another type of roof construction predominated in the later Middle Ages. In this the rafters are supported and stiffened by longitudinal beams called 'side purlins'. These may be supported either by massive secondary rafters on each tie-beam truss or by posts or struts from the beams, or by being morticed directly into the sides of the principal rafters. In a large building such as the barn at Great Coxwell (page 31) there would be two (occasionally three) such longitudinal beams. The illustration is of the roof of a house re-erected at the Avoncroft museum (page 122).

36

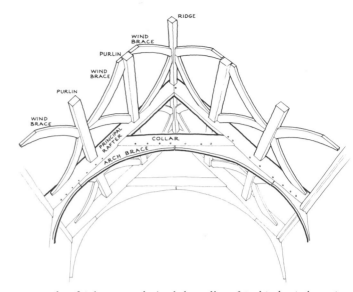

Another form of roof construction, responsible for perhaps the finest and most ornamental roofs is known as the 'arch-braced' roof. In this the tie-beam is eliminated, and instead great curving braces run from the top-plate to meet underneath the centre of the collar.

The photograph is of the roof of the Infirmary at Woodspring Priory (National Trust). It shows the very careful splicing in of new timber and the richness and complexity of the cusped type of decoration characteristic of the West but rarely found in the East. A similar roof but on the grander scale (Guesten Hall) can be seen under repair at the Avoncroft museum, and another roof is being restored by the D.o.E. at Fiddleford Mill, Dorset.

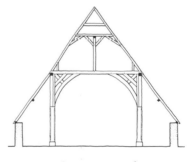

Crown-post roof
with aisles:
St Mary's Hospital,
Chichester.

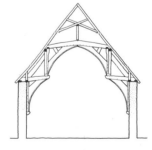

Hammerbeam
roof:
Pilgrims' Hall,
Winchester.

Part of the Pilgrims' Hall roof, Winchester. In the fourteenth century another form of roof construction, which came to be known by the term 'hammer-beam' appears to have been developed first in the South-East, the Pilgrims' Hall being one of the earliest examples to survive. It can be thought of as derivative from aisled construction, the lower, inconvenient part of the aisle-post being eliminated by heavy bracing from the wall; the connecting beam (hammer-beam) supports the truncated top part of the aisle-post.

A small cottage at Newenden in Kent, saved from demolition and restored by local residents. This illustrates the transitional stage between the very small cottage with at the most a loft at one end of the open living-space to a full two-storeyed one; the actual height of the first storey wall from jetty to eaves is barely three feet.

the photographs and line drawings on pages 35–7. Their distribution seems to follow clearly defined patterns, ranging from areas where they are dominant to those where they are almost non-existent. These patterns appear also to correlate with decorative forms, and this has given rise to the idea that there were major schools of carpentry with strong regional loyalties and affiliations, one centred on the North, one on the West, and the third on the South-East. Correlation with dating also supports the idea of rival schools expanding their influence at one period, but in retreat at another.

The Jetty

Structurally the most important innovation during the Middle Ages was the jetty – that is the jettying out in timber

buildings of the upper storey, or storeys, by extending the floor joists so that they project beyond the wall on which they rest, and then supporting the wall above on their projecting ends. This seems to have occurred some time before the end of the thirteenth century and was well established as a new fashion by the fourteenth. It seems most likely that it spread from London, and may have been introduced by merchants of the Hanseatic League who had an important trading centre with wharves and warehouses on the river. Recent excavations of the medieval wharf area in the Hanseatic city of Bergen have revealed at the lowest level (twenty feet below the present surface) jettied buildings of the twelfth century. In the built-up areas of cities the jetty had obvious advantages. It increased the accommodation in

Timber frame of jettied three-storey town house. On the ground floor is the workshop, a counter facing the street and, in the rear bay, an open hearth forming a 'smoke bay' rising through all three floors to the roof. This is now awaiting re-erection at the Weald and Downland Museum, and a reconstruction drawing is shown on page 87.

Upper hall with continuous jetty, as re-erected at the Weald and Downland Museum.

the upper rooms without interfering with the width of the street below. It also provided some shelter and protection to the latter. In the country, however, it is a different matter, and when we find, as we do, isolated houses of the fourteenth century with jetties, some other explanation is needed. The tendency to imitate what had become useful and fashionable in the city would play its part, but there could also have been a structural advantage in stiffening the floor joists by the tension created by the weight carried on

the ends projecting over the supporting walls – a cantilever effect. This could have been the reason for the earliest jetties in rural areas which seem to have been end-jetties, whether in market towns or in isolated farmhouses. Aesthetic considerations, however, soon began to affect its further development, and a type of house to which the name 'Wealden' has been given was evolved in the South-East of England. In this a front jetty and open hall were combined by recessing the hall between jetties on either side. The drawings on page 40 illustrate how this was done.

Bayleaf farmhouse from the central Weald, re-erected at the Weald and Downland Museum. The name 'Wealden' has been given to this type of house in which the open hall is recessed between jettied bays at each end under one continuous roof. The diagrams illustrate the basic structure.

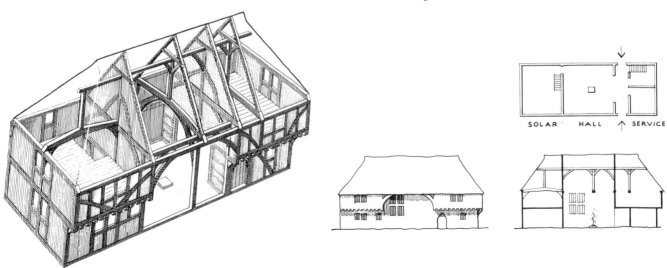

SOLAR   HALL   ↑ SERVICE

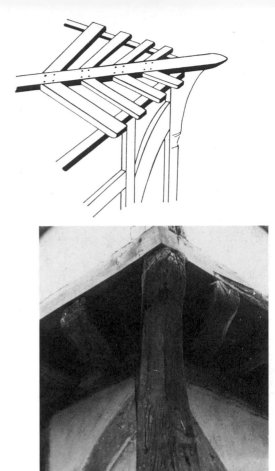

Areas with greatest concentration of 'Wealden' type houses

When, as in the above example, the jetty was carried round on adjacent sides of a building (see also page 112) it was necessary for the ends of the projecting floor joists on which the walls of the upper floor rested to project on both sides. This was achieved by setting a beam diagonally to the corner post which was fitted with a bracket or curved naturally outwards to give stability and rigidity to the jointing. These were called dragon beams and dragon posts, 'dragon' being a corruption of the word 'diagonal'. In order to make even the spacing of the projecting joists they were set at diminishing angles to the dragon beam as illustrated in the diagram. When posts such as these dragon posts or the main bay posts in a building required a larger head to accommodate additional joints or to serve as a bracket, it was usual to get these from the base of tree trunks where the roots spread outwards – hence the use of the word 'rootstock' to describe posts of this kind.

In the cities, most notably in London, the principle of the jetty was employed upwards, in storey above storey, and in the sixteenth century five-storeyed dwellings and workshops with four superimposed jetties were not uncommon, so that houses on opposite sides of the street sometimes gave additional support to each other by connecting beams, only two or three feet in length from gable to gable. In spite of all the precautions taken and the warnings given, fire eventually destroyed utterly what had become both a timber warren and one of the wonders of the world. Our knowledge of

41

Two long terraces with continuous jetties at Stratford-upon-Avon. The further terrace of small houses is dominated by the elaborate chimneys which by the sixteenth century mark the abandonment of the open hearths of the Middle Ages.

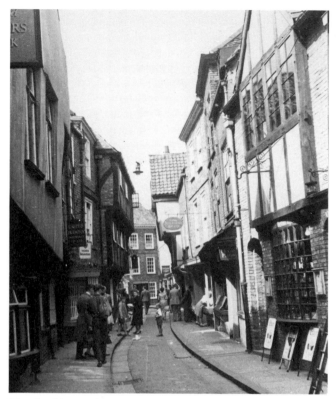

The Shambles, York. An assortment of jettied houses. The gables at the end of the street are separated by only a few feet.

what had been London depends solely on numerous drawings and engravings made during the century before the Great Fire. In the countryside development upwards was not necessary.

By the end of the fifteenth century, long continuous jettying of the first-floor became widely adopted. In houses, the main room – the equivalent of the open hall – was usually at first-floor level in such buildings, but the roof trusses were still exposed as a decorative feature and frequently were further decorated by painting, and, instead of an open central hearth, a chimney at the side or occasionally at the end, of the room.

The jettied upper hall was also favoured in buildings serving some public purpose such as guildhalls, courtrooms or market halls. The jetty gave such upper rooms space and dignity, and in public building the ground floor could be used for various purposes such as storage, stables, workshops, or, in the case of market halls with an open arcade below, a shelter where the officers appointed to control the market and levy tolls could carry on administration with an uninterrupted view of the market place.

The hey-day of the jetty is roughly the period between 1500 and 1650, and its subsequent decline is connected with the increased use of brick and stone. The Fire of London probably did much to accelerate the abandonment of timber as a principal building material, though other factors are often cited – such as the exhaustion of timber resources or the enthusiasm for brick engendered by the latter's use in many of the great buildings of the Tudor period.

Jointing

Some attention has been given recently to methods of timber jointing; in other words, where two or more pieces of wood are joined together, the techniques used to prevent them slipping apart under strain. The purpose of a joint is to resist the tensions and pressures most likely to occur. The simplest example is that of splicing together two beams to form a single length of timber, such as a bottom or top plate, in which the stress is longitudinal, or lateral. In more complicated joints, such as the meeting of post, tie-beam, top plate and rafter, a complex series of pressures and thrusts can develop, so that a more elaborate system had to be evolved. Ideally a joint was so designed that the tenons and mortices provided an interlocking system which would remain stable even without the additional security of pegs driven into holes bored through the interlocking members. Certainly no carpenter would normally rely on subterfuges such as nails, metal straps or ties except to repair original jointing when this has failed – usually through rot or subsidence rather than through insufficient strength.

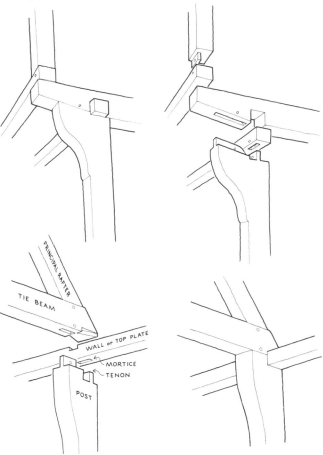

The jettied end of the market hall re-erected at the Weald and Downland Museum and diagrams illustrating the series of interlocking joints.

As in other aspects of building, methods of jointing followed an evolutionary pattern. Like the masons, carpenters were in close contact, and the adoption of new techniques where they had proved superior, seems to have been fairly rapid. On the other hand, some jointing methods tried and proved remained unchanged as long as timber-framing continued. For some areas, such as Essex, the chronology of change has been worked out with a degree of exactness by using firmly dated buildings as a control, in the same way that types of moulding, stops and other forms of decoration have been given reasonably secure dating sequences. In default of a more exact system such as may eventually be provided by dendrochronology, it is only by a combination of such details as these with general data based on structural form, plan, etc., that anything approaching accurate dating of our simpler buildings is possible. Dates inscribed on small or average-sized buildings are very rarely found before the seventeenth century.

As a corollary to the elaborate system of interlocking joints it followed that the erection of the frames of timber buildings could only be done in a definite order. It was not possible to fit in secondary timbers such as braces or intermediate studs, since they had to be tenoned into mortices in the principal timbers, and to be inserted, as assembly proceeded. In most houses and small buildings the timbers would be manhandled and the heavy timbers raised by block and tackle suspended from an easily movable tripod suspended over the structure.

The wattle and daub infilling between the timber framework was sprung in by means of a sliding groove cut into the bottom timber, one end of the pointed stave being inserted first into holes drilled in the underside of the top, the other slid sideways into the groove. Thus nails or any other fixing was unnecessary. In details of this kind there are often

Hoisting into position of a tie-beam from a fifteenth-century upper hall at the same museum by means of block and tackle; the projecting tenon on the top of the left-hand post can be clearly seen.

Manhandling the top-plate of an eighteenth-century granary building at the Weald and Downland Open Air Museum. The projecting tenons of the posts and the brace have to be manoeuvred into the mortices in the underside of the top-plate.

interesting and surprising local differences. The daub mixture itself depended on the loam available, although in all cases a large amount of straw and cow dung seems to have been used in order to bind the material together, prevent cracking, and to give it waterproofing qualities. As much as fifty per cent of straw and dung seems to have been not un-

usual. The wattle, which was woven between the upright staves, was usually of cleft oak or split hazel twigs — occasionally split chestnut. Quite consistently, it appears, oak staves and laths were used for the outside walls, and hazel laths for the less exposed interior partitions. In a great many buildings the original wattle and daub has remained intact in

Woven wattle panels ready to be 'daubed'; top left, the laths are of cleft oak; the bottom panel is of hazel. Oak was used for the heavier, upright staves.

In some cases the staves were inserted horizontally instead of vertically. In this example of a barn at St Fagans Open Air Museum the wattle was not daubed, and this occasionally seems to have been practised where a solid wall was not considered necessary. Another example of an undaubed wall can be seen in the Treadwheel building at the Weald and Downland Museum (page 80).

Although woven wattle was usual, the above form is occasionally found. In this the cleft oak laths are tied by bramble withies instead of being woven. These withies, after four centuries, have the strength and hardness of wire. Variations in technique often occur in areas quite close to each other. A few miles to the east of the area from which these examples are taken nails were normally used to attach the laths to the staves — probably because it was in the middle of an iron-working region.

individual panels from the time when the house was built — a matter of four or five hundred years. This is remarkable testimony to the efficiency of this method of walling, given that the ingredients are right.

All these kinds of timber construction so briefly described can be found combined with stone or, later, with brick. In parts of the South-West houses are frequently encased between stone side walls which may include chimneys; or a timber-frame may rest on a lower storey of stone. There are many examples where a front is stone and all the rest timber-framed. This form of mixed construction should not be confused with the very general re-façading of timber houses which took place all over the country, particularly in the eighteenth century, when timber seems to have been at a discount and was regarded as an inferior, rather low-class material. Up to the end of the sixteenth century timber as a building material does not seem to have been held noticeably lower in prestige than stone. The use of either was a matter of availability. In most highland areas there was no alternative, but where stone and timber were equally accessible there does not seem to have been any obvious preference.

Building in Stone

Unlike timber, stone varies enormously in texture, colour and tractability; and local masons by trial and error adopted techniques of building and decoration most appropriate to the native stone. The earliest, though not necessarily the simplest, in terms of craftsmanship, is what is known as 'dry-

Dry-stone walling and doorway of a longhouse reconstructed at the Highland Museum at Kingussie. Note the thickness of the wall and lowness of the stone lintel.

Merchant's House, Plymouth. Saved from destruction and now open as a museum. Particularly in towns of the South-West the encasing of timber buildings between massive walls of stone became normal in the sixteenth century, often being built above a ground-floor storey of stone. In this case the wall is exposed, and the chimney encased in the wall can be seen.

Farmshed and barn of dry-stone walling on the Cotswold farm of ancient farm breeds, near Stow-on-the-Wold in the Cotswolds. Here some clay bedding is used as mortar, but basically it is a continuation of the dry-stone tradition. Note the way in which the Cotswold-stone tiling is carefully graded from the lower courses to the small tiles near the ridge.

stone' walling. In this no mortar is used, and the stability of the building depends entirely on the skill with which stone (often undressed) is fitted together. The best work, which is possibly in a tradition going back to the Iron Age, is finely jointed, and is made weather-proof, the slope of the stones being so devised as to shed all water. Between this unmortared stone, and carefully coursed and mortared stone, there is an intermediate range in which clay, moss etc., is used as packing. Most surviving buildings of this kind are to be found in the West and South-West, and are farm buildings rather than domestic ones.

Part of the wall of a seventeenth-century mill re-erected at the Weald and Downland Museum. The corners are built of squared lower-greensand stone, and the rest of the wall of roughly trimmed stone. The joints are 'galetted' with small fragments of stone set in the mortar. The stonework is halfway between uncoursed rubble building and finer ashlar.

Mortared stone ranges from random rubble construction to finely cut and regularly coursed ashlar work (see page 122). The dictionary definition of ashlar is 'squared, hewn stone'; like other definitions it is not possible to draw an exact line between carefully controlled and shaped rubble and roughly hewn ashlar. In many cases where coarse stone and freestone – of which the dictionary definition is 'fine grain, easily sawn sandstone or limestone' – are available, we find the latter used for ashlar facade, but more often simply for corners, jambs and lintels. In other areas where softer stone and hard and fine stone are equally obtainable, the exterior skin of a building may be hard, weather-resisting

A much weathered wall of the ruins of the Maison Dieu, or medieval hostel, at Arundel. On the lower section the flint skin has come away, revealing the thick chalk lining. The corner is formed of blocks of lower-greensand stone, in this case easily brought by river from quarries some miles to the north.

stone and the inside of the walls and all interior partitions of the softer stone. In the chalk areas, for example, we frequently find a flint skin, and behind this skin chalk blocks or rubble for the main fabric, with all partitions in chalk.

Building in Cob

The most significant structural feature of cob is that by its nature it needs to be extremely solid at the base, tapering upwards. This produces a 'batter' or slope in the wall so that houses may seem to be out of plumb, or even in danger of collapse if one is not aware of the reason. Provided the assumed need for verticality can be forgotten, this slight leaning back can be felt as an attractive quality giving a greater, rather than a diminished sense of solidity and stability.

Building in Brick

A material which, when introduced, influenced structure considerably is brick – mainly in the design and complexity of chimneys. At first brickmakers and bricklayers followed

'Clay lump' walling in Suffolk. This is a kind of halfway stage between shaped stone and cob. The blocks are made of a mixture of baked clay, stone and straw, and then used as stone might be used, in regular courses, mortared together.

Barn and farm buildings built of cob and converted to other uses at the Sheldon centre in Devon. The tapering irregularity of the walls can be seen clearly in the door and window openings of the buildings to the left.

Looking up the wattle and daub chimney canopy in the fifteenth-century house from Bromsgrove re-erected at the Avoncroft Museum of Buildings.

Head of chimney dated 1636 (Pendean farmhouse, Weald and Downland Museum).

End of chimney-stack, at Erringham in Sussex; late sixteenth or early seventeenth century.

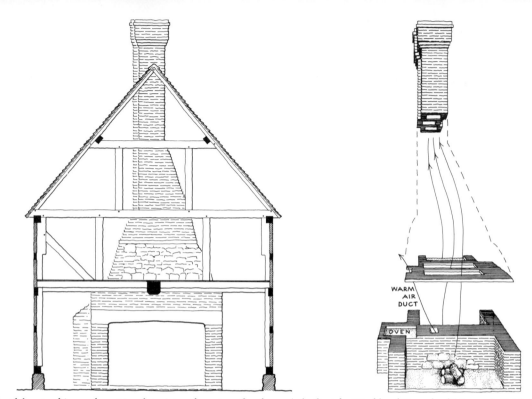

Diagram of the elaborate chimney breast in a late sixteenth-century farmhouse (rebuilt at the Weald and Downland Museum). Brick is for the most part used, but wherever possible local stone for the less intricate portions. An interesting feature is the air-duct between the back-to-back inglenooks, which presumably conducted warmed air to a drying cupboard or enclosed space on the first floor. Eight years ago this appeared to be a unique feature, but since then an identical chimney has been discovered in a house ten miles away during reconstruction. This is the kind of thing which normally escapes detection, but once looked out for, begins to be found elsewhere.

the structural and decorative forms evolved by the masons, and often the moulded surrounds to windows and doors were plastered to simulate stone. The greater flexibility of brick for the construction of chimneys was very soon realised, and it is especially in the great chimneys and fireplaces that brickwork achieves structural and decorative characteristics springing from its special qualities as a building material. The variety in the design of chimneys built in the period between roughly 1500 and 1650 is endless, and the sense of style and fitness has never been bettered. This applies to the humblest cottage perhaps even more than to the more ostentatious designs of the greater mansions.

Recommended Further Reading

C.A. HEWETT, *The Development of Carpentry, 1200–1700*.
   This is concerned entirely with details of carpentry, particularly of jointing and the working out of chronological sequences deduced from firmly dated buildings. Very clearly written and illustrated.

M.J. SWANTON (Editor), *Medieval Domestic Architecture*.
   In this symposium published by the Royal Archaeological Institute a particularly valuable chapter (J.T. Smith's) discusses the distribution of various decorative and structural forms and the evidence for regionally based traditions or 'schools of carpentry'.

Plans and Planning

Origins

In the Introduction mention was made of work done by archaeologists on deserted Saxon village sites, notably at Mucking in the Thames estuary, at Chalton in the Hampshire Downs, at West Stow in Suffolk and at Catholme by the river Trent. This has revealed a very wide distribution of a basic Saxon house plan. In broad outline it is very close to farmhouses of average size surviving from Middle Ages — some fifteen to eighteen feet in width and thirty to forty feet in length, with opposing doorways and a cross-passage. There is often evidence for a partition some six or seven feet from the end of the building, and this space was sometimes divided into two roughly equal parts. This corresponds to the typical medieval open hall with central hearth, cross-passage, and, beyond the cross-passage a buttery and pantry for storage. What we do not know is whether the cross-passage plan which seems to have such remote ancestry was in fact based on its use as a threshing floor with a through draught for winnowing threshed corn. If this was so, when did it cease to be normal and separate barns with threshing floors take its place? It is certain that by the later Middle Ages this use of the cross-passage had ceased over most of the country, although it still continued in extremely remote areas such as the Highlands even up to the twentieth century. Elsewhere only the term 'threshold' continued to point to its original purpose. The retention of the cross-passage is a remarkable example of the persistence and strength of tra-dition, since it is difficult to see what use it continued to serve once its original function was abandoned.

To return to the archaeological evidence for the Saxon house, although there is similarity in plan, there is uncertainty as to height, and whether or not there may have been a second storey at one or both ends, or at least a boarded loft. At Chalton the majority of buildings were of this pattern, with a few scattered sunken huts. Although there is no evidence for the sunken-hut method of building after the Norman conquest one can hazard a conjecture that the smallest type of one-roomed medieval cottage or workshop, consisting simply of one bay if timber-built, was its later equivalent in status and use, and that the larger form with its cross-passage was the prototype of the more substantial houses of the later Middle Ages.

The Open Hearth

For the whole of the Saxon period the house plan, without apparently any exception, centred on the open hearth with a general living space round it. After the Norman conquest this continued up to the end of the fifteenth century to be the normal house plan for perhaps 90 per cent of the population. Whether at the top or bottom of the social pyramid life centred on the open hearth. Above the hearth the roof-structure was not closed in by any ceiling and it provided vents or 'louvres' to release the smoke. The loftier the roof

Reconstruction of a thirteenth-century croft at Ryedale Folk Museum. It consists of one room with a central hearth. It is larger than the reconstruction of the thirteenth-century flint-built cottage at the Weald and Downland Museum, and without a partition. Page 13.

space the freer from smoke would be the living space and the less the danger from fire. The roof being illuminated by flames from wood burning on the open hearth, and by any subsidiary lighting from tapers, became a feature for decorative treatment, giving grandeur and splendour to the greater houses, and some sense of dignity and aesthetic satisfaction to the smaller. A feeling for good proportion and care in design characterise even the smaller cottages and houses that survive from the Middle Ages, however limited the resources for additional decoration. Whether we have to thank the strong craft traditions of the carpenters or masons who carried out the work, or the general quality of feeling and sensibility of the society in which they worked, or the individuals for whom the houses were designed, we cannot tell; we can only recognise such qualities.

The living room or 'hall', therefore, with its open hearth was the first essential. Probably a large percentage of the smaller cottages consisted of this and nothing more.

Differences in Size and Number of Rooms

Between the small single-roomed cottage, simple in construction and plan, and the manor houses with perhaps two-storeyed accommodation at both ends of the hall, there were a large number of possible intermediate stages, and various forms of elaboration. Interior plans grade into each other and there are no essential distinctions between one stage and the next. The simple cottage with a flimsy partition between hall and storage area developed into the two-roomed cottage with full division and door; the shelf or rudimentary loft at eaves level became a substantially constructed floor with sleeping and storage accommodation, and ladder

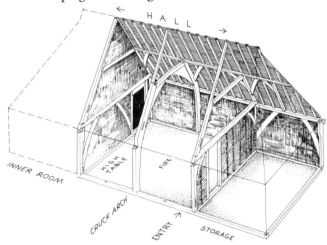

Drawing of a single-storey house re-erected at the Weald and Downland Museum, late medieval in date. The hall is given space and dignity by the use of base crucks. Although of one storey it adheres to the three-bay house plan with cross-passage and service wing at the lower end and a parlour at the higher or dais end.

access; this in turn became partitioned off and the walls raised, enabling a low window to light the upper storey; and so to the final stage, with a first floor equal in height to the lower storey and the windows of the open hall rising through the equivalent of two storeys up to the eaves. The latter is certainly the standard accommodation that those of medium status in the community – such as the growing yeoman farmer class – expected in the South-East by the end

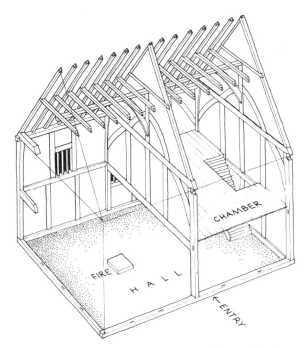

Drawing of a two-storey house also re-erected at the Weald and Down-land Museum. In this example the hall occupies the whole of two bays, but one of these is floored over, providing an upper room or solar in that half. There are buildings of similar size and construction (in the same Wealden area) in which the hall occupies only one of the two bays, the other bay being partitioned off, giving two rooms, presumably service below and solar above.

of the fourteenth century. In remoter regions in the North and West expectations might not reach this stage even by the eighteenth century, if then.

In most areas, and throughout the Middle Ages, cottages and farms at all these different stages of elaboration were almost certainly being built in every area and in most village communities – the degree of elaboration being simply a matter of the relative wealth of the area or status of the individual. The only generalisation that it is safe to make is that certain variants of plan became established in a given area at a particular period or among a particular class in the community.

The Linear Plan

The kind of elaboration that took place in this country was limited and perhaps simplified by the early abandonment of the aisled form of construction. After the thirteenth century aisles were almost entirely confined to non-domestic building. As a result, the size of the roof unsupported by intermediate posts restricted the width of most buildings to some seventeen or eighteen feet. Anything beyond that involved very heavy tie-beams and massive rafters, greatly increasing the cost of building, even if such large timbers were readily available. Few, in fact, of the Saxon parish churches exceed this width and it was only when carpenters devised better methods of supporting the roof structure that a span of more than fourteen or fifteen feet became frequent in houses below manorial status.

Development of the house plan, therefore, had to be linear – an increase in length rather than in width, quite unlike the kind of wide and spacious farmsteads to be seen in many areas from which our Saxon ancestors came. In these areas, so far from being rejected, the aisled form, or roof structures

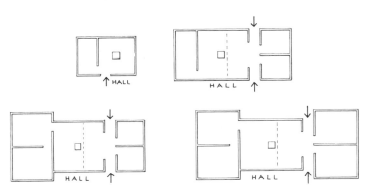

This sequence of drawings shows the evolution from the simple single room with an all-purpose living room and hall, to the final six-roomed house of two storeys. In practice there could be many intermediate stages and variations in the proportions of the rooms and the role played by each part, but so long as the bay form of construction persisted and the roof remained open and was regarded as a principal decorative feature, any increase in accommodation had to be linear.

supported by interior posts or partitions, became dominant. In aisleless structures additional rooms could only be added to either end of the hall. If very large rooms were needed, it was found in practice more convenient, and possibly more aesthetically attractive, for these to be built at right-angles in the form of 'cross wings' with separate roof structure. Such cross wings did not need to be restricted in length, which was frequently greater than that of the hall, and were often divided into two rooms. A further extension of the linear plan could include under one roof byres and general storage space, with direct access from the lower end of the hall. The term 'longhouse' has been given to this type of plan. It had great advantages in cold or difficult climatic conditions; but

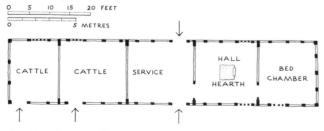

This fifteenth-century house of a modified longhouse plan and of cruck construction, has been re-erected at St Fagans Museum. The domestic part is at the far end in the photograph. To fit the strictest definition of a 'longhouse' there would need to be a single entrance for cattle and humans and direct access from house to byre.

in this country has only been found in certain areas of the West and North – some of them in situations such as Upton in the Severn Valley, not particularly exposed to bad weather. If the longhouse ever existed in the South-East it was exceptional; the evidence from deserted village sites points to byres and barns and other storage buildings being separated from domestic buildings. The longhouse and other forms of plan which combine domestic and farm buildings under one roof are considered a little more fully in the next chapter.

Exceptions to the Linear and Open-Hearth Plan
There were two main exceptions to the centralised hearth and hall plan with its linear extensions. One is found in the castles or manor houses built over a stone and usually vaulted undercroft; or in towns where stone houses are frequently built over a semi-basement store. In these the hearths were set against a wall with large canopies, and flues carried up within the wall itself. This was possibly a form of building introduced shortly before the Norman conquest from the Continent. In the Bayeux Tapestry, for example, such a hall over an undercroft seems to be suggested in the scene which represents Harold feasting at Bosham in 1065.

The second exception was probably confined at first to a few cities in congested urban areas. It arose from the need to economise space on limited sites by building upwards. Few surviving buildings of three or more storeys go back beyond the fourteenth century, but there is no reason to suppose that York or London and a few other cities did not contain houses of at least three or possibly four storeys long before that. The merchant house at Exeter which attained notoriety when it was removed bodily to a new site in 1961 is, if correctly dated, a fourteenth-century example of an urban house adapted to an extremely awkward site by a mixture of jettying combined with an irregular ground plan; it rises from a very small base to four storeys if we include the attic. By that time this kind of thing was no doubt commonplace in London.

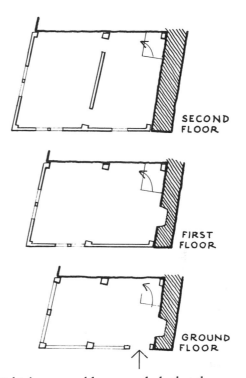

SECOND FLOOR

FIRST FLOOR

GROUND FLOOR

A fourteenth-century merchant's house in Exeter. The drawings show the irregularity of the ground plan and the small area of the ground floor compared with that of the second floor. This house was a centre of great interest in 1961 when as a result of conservation efforts it was saved from demolition and removed without dismantling to a new site a hundred yards away.

It is, I think, reasonable to conclude that the open hearth, wherever practicable, was preferred not only in Saxon times, but throughout the Middle Ages, and that status played little part in its choice. Many of the greater mansions built towards the close of the sixteenth century were still focused on the great hall with its central hearth. The layout of the hall was governed by a tradition tested and perfected by many generations. In the larger houses the 'cross-passage' was often separated by elaborate open-work screens, but the entrances remained on both sides exactly opposite each other, and doors led from the side of the cross-passage into the service rooms – the pantry and the 'buttery' (the latter not a dairy, but a 'butlery' for drink). Sometimes a third opening went to an outside kitchen. At the opposite (or 'upper') end of the hall in the larger houses there might be a small raised platform with a decorated 'dais' beam running across the partition at first-floor level, with a door, or doors, leading into a 'parlour'at ground level, and stairs or a ladder to a solar or upper chamber leading directly from the hall or from behind the partition.

Within this ground plan there was scope for great variation. For example, there might be an upper chamber at the lower end, above the buttery and pantry, projecting over the cross-passage; the latter might be screened from the hall by projecting 'speres'. In addition to the doors leading to the pantry and buttery, there might be a third door between these leading by a passage to an outside kitchen or bake-house. All these openings, the roof structure, the dais beam and other principal timbers provided scope for decoration appropriate to structure and material. The decorative vocabulary on the whole was worked out with great sensitivity and understanding, and the smaller houses did what they could afford to reproduce these decorative features on a reduced scale. Even a very small two-roomed cottage might run to some finely moulded detail.

A striking example of the way in which aesthetic considerations could over-ride purely structural considerations is found in the diversity in width of the bay divisions wherever the hall was large enough to occupy more than one bay. In these cases the upper or dais end bay was usually made longer than the lower bay, for a very good reason. The table at which meals were eaten was situated in front of a bench under the dais beam, and the family sat with their backs to the wall facing the open hearth. The central truss would therefore form a dominant decorative feature, only seen at its best when situated at some distance from the table. Rarely are the upper bays less than twelve feet long, but the lower bays in a medium-sized hall might be much less. In other words, in the interest of appearance, a more efficent structural approach was modified.

The Change from Open Hearth to Enclosed Hearth and Chimney

The smallest cottages, those consisting of one room or one bay only, were probably to be found in every village up to the Tudor period. Few survive in the South-East, and those

that do were probably built by squatters on the edge of common land. In the North and West, particularly in stone areas, they are more numerous. In these the transition to closed hearth and chimney was simple; it could only go at

Crofter's cottage of just one room with an end chimney, restored at the Auchindrain Museum.

the gable end. The transition, however, was probably mediated by a period when the hearth was simply moved from a central position to the end with a rough canopy of wattle and daub and timber-frame to direct the smoke through the roof opening. In the case of timber buildings there was a transitional period when a short end bay with a smoke hood, perhaps not more than four or five feet deep, was built as an integral part of such single-roomed cottages (occasionally of two-roomed cottages) – the complete chimney-breast being inserted much later.

For two-roomed cottages there were alternatives. When built of timber a central chimney near where the open hearth had been was normal. In stone areas it might be at either or both ends, or centrally placed. Whichever it was, it necessitated a change in interior planning. Before the adoption of the closed hearth there was a main living space, and anything else was secondary space; in other words, the division of

A two-roomed cottage restored and furnished as it was when last occupied. The cottage is maintained as a museum by the Pembroke Museums Service.

Cottage of one storey, but with an attic above at eaves level lit by a window in the gable end. Rebuilt in the Ryedale Museum.

space was unequal, but with the adoption of a closed hearth and central chimney the divisions tend to become roughly equal. In two-roomed cottages it is this plan which has persisted in most parts of Great Britain. They are normal for the crofters' cottages of the Highlands or the smallholders' cottages in Ireland, or, to take a more specialised group, the thousands of toll cottages erected for the gatekeepers of the new Turnpike system in the eighteenth and early nineteenth centuries. The room division in these two-roomed cottages was ordinarily roughly equal, unlike the very unequal divisions of hall and storage (or service rooms) of the medieval cottages.

Loft Space and Ceilings

In many cases the attic space above the eaves was floored, either when the house was built or at a later date; and in some areas there was an external stair and entry to this upper storage space. There is, however, no line that can be clearly drawn between, (a) the interior loft at eaves level at one end of a small cottage with its open hearth, (b) the completely closed loft with exterior stair and door, and (c) a complete two-storeyed treatment at one end. The chain of development was continuous and every house was subject to adaptation, conversions or extensions.

Although the single- or two-celled cottage with open hearth and roof was probably the norm for the majority of the rural population, the larger, three-celled fully developed two-storeyed hall was, as we have seen, normal for at least the middle and upper sections of the community, and it is at this level that the transition from the open hearth to chimney-breast began, and where we can clearly see how gradual it was. Of all the changes in interior planning that have taken place, the substitution of the enclosed fireplace for the open hearth could be regarded as the most dramatic and revolutionary. Yet even this took place by degrees — in most places a stage-by-stage development during two or three generations. The new fashion seems to have been adopted from the Continent — probably through increasing contact with the Netherlands, where chimneys were rapidly displacing open hearths before this took place in this country. The first stage was usually to move the hearth from near the centre to the lower end of the hall, and to set it against a reredos; then to seal over the upper part of the hall but leave open as a smoke-bay that part where the fire was now placed. The next stage might be to confine the hearth to a corner and build a canopy to channel the smoke through a

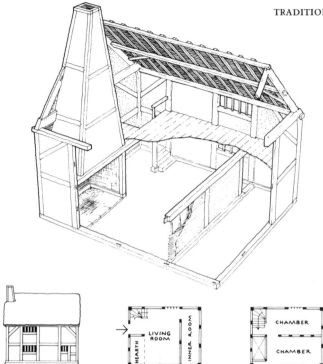

Drawing of an early seventeenth-century cottage rebuilt by the Central Electricity Generating Board at Coleshill and now part of a Field and Local Studies Centre; an example of the transitional phase between a central open hearth and a closed chimney breast. The hearth occupies one half of a small end bay with a timber-frame wattle and daub 'chimney' or canopy above. In other houses similar in plan but perhaps rather earlier in date, the narrow end bay might have been a smoke bay without any canopy or chimney with the stairs to the upper floor within this open smoke bay.

Wattle and daub hood over a hearth built against a simple straight stone reredos or wall in a re-erected cruck-framed cottage at Ryedale Museum. This can be regarded as a stage between the completely open hearth near the centre of the living room or hall, and the enclosed inglenook. It is a stage nearer the latter than the open smoke bay or the hood supported on posts.

smaller opening and perhaps at the same time to extend the floor of the room which already covered most of the hall. Only then might a chimney-breast – the final stage in the transition – be inserted. What is significant is that each of these transitional stages was sufficiently long-drawn-out, and apparently accepted as a satisfactory arrangement, for new houses to be built in that way. What we might perhaps call the 'smoke-bay' era lasted in many areas for at least half a century. In the South-East the transition was virtually com-

plete by the end of the sixteenth century. By that time almost all houses, including even the smallest cottages, were being built from the outset with chimneys, often of exceedingly elaborate design, although a few houses with open hearths and halls continued to be built by conservatives. This was the situation in the South-East, and roughly the same pattern followed later in the West, the North, and finally the Scottish Highlands. In the Hebrides, farmhouses with central open hearths were still being built in the nineteenth century, and continued to be lived in without chimneys up to a few years ago (see page 140).

A number of factors no doubt played their part. Before the end of the fifteenth century the open halls had already been diminishing in size relative to the rooms at either end.

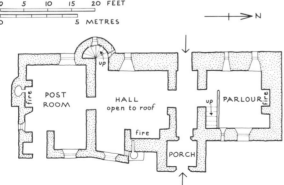

The Old Post Office at Tintagel, fifteenth-century. The semi-circular turret staircase projects from the middle of the rear wall. The hall part is open to the roof which is massive but rather roughly carpentered compared with work farther to the east. The plan indicates the immense thickness of the slate walls, and the weight of the tiles is shown in the photograph by the sagging of the roof between trusses.

Whereas truckle beds and box-beds would have been the normal sleeping accommodation in the hall, the movement towards a more individual and private mode of living spurred a drive towards more personal accommodation such as bedrooms, withdrawing rooms and libraries. These rooms were increasingly sought after by the upper classes, and they set the fashion. The division of the hall created more rooms and the great inglenook fireplaces gave protection from draughts in what may have been worsening climatic conditions during this period – which is sometimes referred to as 'the little ice age'. The symbol of the cave became more acceptable than that of the campfire.

Another development associated with the horizontal division of the floor in the medium-sized two-storey building was the addition of a small projecting wing to accommodate a staircase. In the South these usually take the form of a square 'vyse' with a wooden newel staircase, but in stone areas, particularly in the North and South-West, they may take the form of a semi-circular or 'turret' stair. This was nothing new; it had been a common device in castles and church towers, but it got a new lease of life and was adopted in buildings of a much lower status.

Rooms and their Uses

A question difficult to answer is how these new rooms should be described and what were the uses to which they were put. It is not a new question. The standard medieval plan is given as 'parlour' at ground level and 'solar' above, with 'buttery' and 'pantry' at the lower or 'service' end, also with a chamber above. The open hall and service rooms are not in question, but all the other rooms are. Only occasionally inventories may help by listing the furniture in a room, but there is very little consistency, and as often as not it is impossible to be certain which rooms are being referred to. The name 'solar' for the most graciously designed room after the hall, seems to be derived from a French phrase, meaning 'under the eaves' rather than from the Latin for 'sun' or for 'solitude'. As a room it probably often served two quite different purposes – as a sleeping or guest chamber during the summer, and for storage in winter, somewhat

59

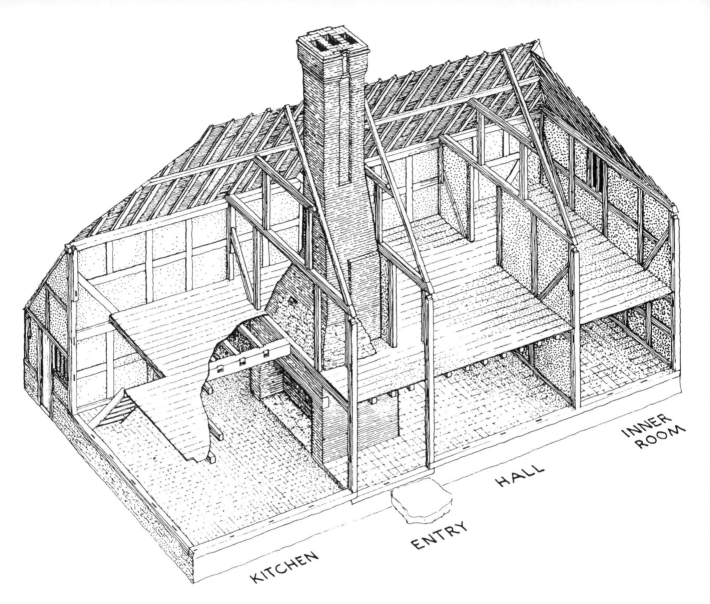

KITCHEN

ENTRY

HALL

INNER ROOM

Drawing of a farmhouse, built about 1600 and re-erected at the Weald and Downland Museum: it illustrates the completion of the transition from open hall to inglenook chimney-breast. The elaborate chimney is integral to the building as are the floors, stairs and partitions, but we could take out the chimney which occupies roughly the space that would have been the cross-passage, and remove the floor of the central bay and be left with a plan and structure indistinguishable from that of a fifteenth-century house with open hall and hearth. It is difficult to give names to the rooms in the new interior plan. From left to right, living room (kitchen), parlour (hall), store room or dairy (inner room) would perhaps be appropriate. The chimney breast includes back-to-back inglenooks, the one on the left being slightly larger, with an oven and hanging bars for cauldrons; but there is no room which equates to the medieval solar. This plan became a fairly standard one for three-celled houses. The chimney is illustrated in detail on page 50, the exterior on page 96.

analogous to the 'stuas' of Scandinavian farmsteads, though very differently positioned. Even the hall and the use of the open hearth is ambiguous when cooking is considered. How far was cooking done in the hall, or in an external kitchen or bakehouse? Was it simply a matter of size and status? The name 'parlour' is generally given to the room below the solar leading off the hall at the upper end. This again suggests a quite misleading comparison with the standard 'parlour' and 'kitchen-living' room of the great majority of cottages and small houses from the eighteenth to the twentieth centuries.

Just as in the larger houses the transition from open hearth to inglenook by the division of the open hall, horizontally, and sometimes vertically, created more rooms without necessarily extending the size of the ground plan, so in the smaller houses we find a remarkable number of two-storeyed cottages with central, side or end chimneys being built during this period and occupying no more space than the small single-storeyed cottages. The ground coverage is often not more than a twenty-feet frontage by a twelve-feet depth. These cottages can be found all over the southern half of England dating from the end of the sixteenth to the middle of the seventeenth centuries. How far we can regard these 'two up and two down' four-roomed cottages as the 'up-to-date' successors of earlier single-storeyed cottages, or for what classes in a community they were built, is not easy to decide; but they do seem to represent a very general upgrading of accommodation and standard of housing – part of the 'great rebuilding', a phrase often used to describe this period. In these houses all four rooms are virtually identical in size. Techniques of building, however, did not change to the same extent. There is little difference in the methods of construction of timber houses or in the work of the mason; there may be nothing to distinguish the framing of a house of the fifteenth century which has had a chimney inserted from one built at the beginning of the seventeenth century with chimney, floor, stairs and partitions integral to the building. Some decorative details may be modified and less care given to the carpentry of the roof which became no longer of visual importance. Even in a house sufficiently 'advanced' to

include glazed casement windows these would normally correspond in their positioning and size to the unglazed openings of previous centuries. It is not until the next century that such details of proportion and placing became generally altered following the fashion being set by buildings outside the definitions of traditional and vernacular.

There were also some secondary changes in this later period. For example, with the gradual substitution of coal for wood as fuel (in cities such as London even before the end of the Middle Ages), the need for smaller grates and hearths led not only to smaller flues and chimney stacks, but to the enclosure of the wide and deeply recessed inglenooks of the sixteenth and seventeenth centuries, turning them into cupboard spaces or just hollow recesses. In recent years these tend to be uncovered again with our changing attitudes towards interior space and room design.

One unanswered question remains. Almost all these great inglenook chimney breasts, whether in newly built houses

Kitchen at Donnington-le-Heath manor, restored and furnished as a museum by the Leicester Museums Service. The furnishing of the kitchen has been particularly well done, down to rushes scattered on the floor. The hearth and chimney is built against and into the stone wall. In the greater establishments the kitchen would be separate, but in small or great, the hall – the living centre of the house – would have an open hearth.

or inserted into existing medieval open halls, incorporate ovens. This is so in quite small cottages, as well as in larger isolated farmhouses. It is inconceivable that the oven was an innovation of the Tudor period; the evidence from deserted medieval village sites such as Hangleton suggests that the oven was just as normal a feature of each individual house or cottage in the thirteenth century as it was in the seventeenth century. Some of the houses at Hangleton had, in fact, two ovens. We therefore have to assume that the average medieval house with its open hearth usually had an oven, or bakehouse-cum-kitchen, in a separate building outside. Traces of these are very rarely found, and the only explanation must be that when these external kitchens and ovens became redundant, they were not suited for adaptation to any other purpose (analogous, in fact to the fate of the external earth-closet some three centuries later). The only other possible explanation might be that the average small village community depended on a communal bakehouse – a system which seems to have continued in parts of northern France up to the nineteenth century; but at present such evidence as there is seems to point to an individual, rather than a communal arrangement in this country.

Building Upwards

Another development found before the end of the sixteenth century is the growing use of the previously open roof space – loft or storage area – into an attic room above the level of the eaves. This might be lit either by a small window in the gable end or, in the more congested environment of village or town, by a dormer window, which was another innovation of this period. Such space might be increased by continuing the wall or lowering the attic floor some three feet. In the case of timber-framed buildings the tie-beam was lowered to support the floor joists and struts inserted to support the roof. As a result we now find cottages of three rooms, one above the other, with chimneys built against the end or the side, and providing hearths in the ground-floor and first-floor rooms. Such cottages may cover a ground area as

Small two-roomed cottage in the Cotswolds. The rooms are vertically arranged, the one over the other, halving the roof area and foundations required.

little as twelve by fourteen feet. It is true that medieval jettied buildings within towns, such as the house in Exeter (page 55), were often as economical of ground space as this, but these cottages can be found in isolated positions. The reason can only be saving of cost in foundations or roofing.

A cottage built probably in the first half of the seventeenth century and waiting re-erection at the Weald and Downland Museum. It has three storeys if we include the garret which is lit by a small window in the gable end. The massive external stone and brick chimney provides flues for the ground and first-floor rooms, and, at its side, the stairs leading to the first floor and attic. Building upwards like this, even on isolated country sites, became not unusual in the seventeenth century.

Town house at Horsham (Sussex), built about 1600. The jettied attic storey is provided with exceptionally large dormer windows which light a large chamber open to the roof – possibly a weaving gallery.

The Terrace and the Semi-Detached

The terrace in the sense of a long series of identical or nearly identical houses built at one time as a single planned development, has a long history, nor was it confined to the larger cities. A number of examples from the fifteenth century survive in quite small towns (see pages 85, 97 and 105). As in so many other changes it is not easy to make any clear distinction between the close building of individual houses in a compactly built street and a terrace organised as a single unit and consisting of identical houses. In fact, early terraces built as one unit were frequently varied in design, while it was quite usual for individual houses to be linked and a common roof structure built or rebuilt across any awkward gaps between one house and the next. All one can say is that we do

Late medieval terrace at Tewkesbury, Gloucestershire. It was probably built by a speculative builder to provide small houses and shops. Its design was made attractive and interesting by the introduction of a three-storeyed unit in the middle. An interesting feature is the accommodation of an open hearth by leaving a part of the structure behind the jettied rooms facing the street open to the roof. This is similar in plan to the late medieval shop now being re-erected at the Weald and Downland Museum, but in the latter example the roof axis runs back from the gable facing the street and is therefore a genuine 'smoke bay'.

The Vicars Close, at Wells: a most remarkable terrace of small houses, surviving from the fourteenth century, but perhaps not vernacular in the strictest sense. The houses have been altered in various ways – doors, windows, interior partitions and extensions at the rear – but the original plan seems to have been identical – a small ground-floor hall with chimney-breast and hearth in the thickness of the stone wall, but projecting a little on the outside; and at the back of the hall a spiral staircase to the room ('solar'? parlour? or bedroom?) above.

Early seventeenth-century terrace at Shepton Mallet (Somerset). These seven houses are identical in plan and structure, but with the usual alterations of windows and unsightly additions. The chimneys are of brick, but the rest is of the grey limestone of that part of the oolitic belt.

Semi-detached houses built of Portland stone ashlar about 1600 in Weymouth; each is the mirror-image of the other; conserved as a local museum and appropriately furnished.

find that the uniform terrace with a considerable number of identical houses became commoner in this period, and in the eighteenth century was given a prestige quality by being adopted in London and such fashionable cities as Bath. It is a form fitted to economical and rapid building, and was adopted in debased versions in the expanding industrial regions. Such terraces of the late eighteenth and early nineteenth centuries still remain in certain respects vernacular and traditional. The simple plan of the two up and two down was almost universal, and local materials and traditional forms of decoration were often retained.

Another new device, the 'semi-detached', consisted of two houses sharing a common dividing wall and continuous roof structure. The earliest examples from the late sixteenth and early seventeenth centuries are often not exact mirror images of each other; the inglenook may be a little larger in one or the decoration more elaborate, or the party-wall may be placed not exactly midway, so that one of the dwellings is slightly larger than the other. There may also be clear evidence of an interconnecting door. A possible explanation of these small differences may be that such houses were built for senior and junior members of one family; just as in the Middle Ages two open halls of different size and quality can often be found adjacent with communicating doors. But in these cases they are invariably of different dates and not planned as a single unit.

Semi-detached farm cottages at the Beamish Open Air Museum. They also provide an example of the 'double-pile' plan in which one roof encompasses rooms back and front, each with separate fireplaces and flues which converge below the centrally placed chimney. The roof covering is of local slate which contrasts with the pantiles on the roof of the stable. Pantiles have been used widely in the eastern parts of England and Scotland from the sixteenth century onwards and appear to have been introduced from the Continent. In many areas the tradition, once established, has remained dominant to the present day. (See page 117.)

Jetties and Interior Planning

We have seen how, in towns, pressure of space had placed a premium on verticality, particularly in cities such as London. Town houses, for reasons of frontage space, were usually aligned away from the street with the gable end of the roof facing the street, and with the principal rooms at first- or even second-floor level, the ground floor often being occupied as workshop or store. In such buildings the rooms on the first and second floor in the jettied façade were both more spacious, lighter and pleasanter, and it was therefore natural that they formed the best apartments and were often the most richly decorated. In these cases fireplaces would be built in the walls at the rear or at the side (see page 46). There were, however, two ways by which the desire for an open hearth could be met. It could be situated on the ground floor within a smoke bay, and open hearths of this kind have been found behind workshops facing the street in towns as far apart as Tewkesbury, Horsham and Sandwich. The second possibility was that of a central hearth actually at first-floor level. That these existed has been established by their remains on plaster or stone bases resting directly on the floor joists.

In the countryside such devices were not necessary, but with the popularity of the continuous jetty in the Tudor period in town and countryside and its coincidence with the abandonment of the open hearth, there was a period, lasting for rather more than half a century, when in the timber building regions of the South and East the principal room was situated not on the ground floor, but at first-floor level. These upper halls were treated with all the lavishness of decoration, and given the importance that had previously been a feature of the medieval open-hearth hall. In some ways the late sixteenth- and early seventeenth-century upper-hall houses can be seen as a kind of reversion to the hall over an undercroft, which was normal in the early Middle Ages when building in stone. The difference was that then it was restricted almost entirely to houses of at least manorial status, but now it was enjoyed by a much larger section of the community.

An interesting and very different interior plan used in this

Looking up at the gallery at first-floor level – half of it built over the hall, and half over the continuous jetty – at the Blue Boar, Winchester.

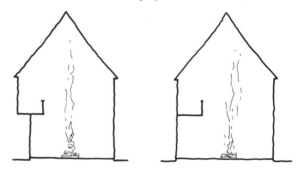

The left-hand section shows the linking gallery connecting rooms at first-floor level at each end of the hall, combined with a continuous jetty as in the Blue Boar, Winchester. On the right is a gallery inserted into a hall at a stage before insertion of floor and chimney.

period of transition has recently been discovered in Winchester. Here a continuous jetty was combined with an open ground-floor hearth and open hall by using the jetty to provide an open walkway along the inside of the hall, conveniently linking the rooms at first-floor level at either end of the hall. It is possible that this device was not unusual and that other examples will be found. The insertion of a gallery to connect the two-storeyed ends of an open hall before the abandonment of the open hearth and the flooring over of the hall has frequently been found as a transitional stage. The incorporation of a jetty as part of such a linking gallery illustrates the gradual step-by-step process by which these transitions were made.

The 'Double Pile' House

With improving standards of accommodation and the demand for more room, another device was used in the seventeenth and more frequently in the eighteenth century. This is the 'double pile' house, in which two parallel roofs, with a drainage valley between, double the depth of a building. Long before the end of the Middle Ages this was to be found in towns where congestion necessitated parallel structures of this kind, with the line of the roofs running back from the street. Normally these were separate houses, but occasionally two or three parallel units might be combined in one large house (see the Merchant's House, Plymouth, page 46 and the Butterwalk, Dartmouth, page 111). Outside the towns such limitation of space is not the reason; but rather the desire for a different kind of interior plan and greater flexibility. This method was fully exploited in some of the greater mansions, but was now applied to the smaller houses and cottages, first to extend, and then as integral to a larger plan. It could, and often did, revolutionise interior planning. The linear plan, either in its horizontal or vertical form gave place to a much

freer apportionment of space, the positioning of stairs, entrance lobbies and so on.

The term double-pile is also rather loosely used to describe any plan in which two principal rooms are set from front to back across the roof's axis. This widening of the roof became possible once the roof structure had ceased to be a matter of aesthetic interest, so that the roof could be supported by interior partitions, posts and struts. The linear form of regular bays and symmetrical and ornamental roof structure no longer had any meaning as soon as ceilings hid it from view. This form of double-pile was adopted very widely in the Midlands and in the North – in the laithe farmhouses, in eighteenth- and nineteenth-century terraces and in semi-detached and small houses. One can find examples where the depth from front to back may be more than twice the frontage, and with standard two-up and two-down accommo-

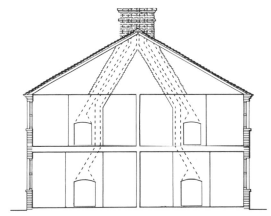

Diagram of 'double-pile' house seen in section.

dation reversed in their relationship to the roof. We can occasionally find examples where double-pile houses using the term in the first sense – of parallel ranges – have been converted to the second form by altering the original double roof to one roof twice the width and twice the height, thus providing useful additional loft space and getting rid of the valley gutter, usually a source of endless trouble through blockages and difficulty of access.

A typical terrace of 'double pile' industrial cottages at the Abbeydale Industrial Hamlet near Sheffield.

67

Outshots and Penthouses

There are two other ways by which an existing house plan could be easily altered. One was by the addition of outshots or penthouses in which the roof line was brought down to enclose a space varying from five to eight feet in width. Such outshots are not necessarily an addition and some have been found which are integral with quite early buildings. Also it is not easy to distinguish an outshot from an aisle. Many aisled barns, for example, are on examination found to have started without aisles; the reverse can also happen – when, for example, an original aisle has been walled up and the aisled space turned into an external lean-to cattle shed. This kind of rearrangement can be easily verified in barns where the structure is completely exposed and mortices for partitions or stave holes can be seen; but it is not so ascertainable in houses. In most cases outshots are later additions, and in some cases both the sides and ends of a building were thus extended, particularly when an earlier house was divided up into two or more cottages (see page 96).

The majority of the smaller traditional houses will be found to fall within these large categories of plan; but as in the use and variety of materials or of construction there are countless local and regional differences, so there are variations in basic plans. Sometimes these are the product of ostentatious individualism, sometimes of genuine experimentation, or adaption to local needs. There are, however, some more impersonal and universal factors which, within the last hundred years, have influenced interior planning and exterior design such as the enforcement of building regulations fixing the minimum height of ceilings, or the area of window space in relation to floor space. Such regulations are made with the best intentions, but when combined with the abandonment of traditional local materials as is happening over the whole of the oolitic belt, including the Cotswold area, local traditions can be given a mortal blow, and the mere control of colour, or height, or some detail of window or door treatment cannot resurrect them.

This photograph illustrates the effect of a change in the height of ceilings and the spacing of windows, otherwise identical, though obviously not original.

Recommended Further Reading

M. BARLEY, *English Farmhouse and Cottage*.
  Deals particularly with interior planning, uses of rooms and furnishings, using inventories and wills, mainly of the sixteenth and seventeenth centuries.

R. HARRIS, *Discovering Timber-Framed Buildings*.
  (Very well illustrated and concise.)
R.T. MASON, *Framed Buildings of England*.

Farmsteads and Farm Buildings

Up to the middle of the eighteenth century the majority of the population was involved in agriculture, even the craftsmen and traders in the market towns combined their main occupation with some agricultural work in the fields outside. In the Middle Ages the parish priest often had holdings in the common fields, and the lord of the manor was actively involved in the way in which agriculture was managed by the community, and not only in the demesne lands attached

Bonsall, Pennine hay-barn. Typical of the mixed use of limestone and sandstone, and of the pattern of small field barns in this case associated with lead mining in this part of the Pennines. Below the hay-loft are usually two or three stalls and feeding racks. These buildings are well constructed, functional and undecorated but fine examples of the traditional skills of the local masons. Now they are mostly derelict.

to the manor. With the decay of the early and more communal forms of management, and with an increased number of independent farmers, this kind of general involvement in agriculture still continued for most of those living in villages and market towns. Inventories of the seventeenth century include many craftsmen and traders owning some livestock or 'corn in the granary' or crops growing in the fields. When we try to discover what kind of buildings met the needs of such small-scale farming, or their relationship to the houses of those who divided their activities in this way, only here and there can we find a tiny barn, granary, wagon-shed or stable converted to store or tool-shed. In a few areas, such as parts of the Pennines where lead miners or cloth workers still divided their time between industry and a few fields until late into the nineteenth century, a pattern of such small buildings and holdings can still be traced, but from such examples it would be unwise to deduce anything about the farming landscape of an earlier period. Few farm buildings survive from before the Tudor period; except for the great barns of the monastic estates and tithe or manorial barns only those of prosperous independent yeoman farmers dating from the fourteenth century onwards can still be found in some areas, and these tell us little about ordinary farm organisation and layout. Other farm buildings are usually of varying dates, and the pattern of building and rebuilding does not necessarily represent an earlier pattern.

Bearing all this in mind it is still possible to trace a few

Cilewent Farmhouse. Re-erected at St Fagans Museum, this is a long-house by the strictest definition, having a single entrance to the byre and house-part. The living quarters lie beyond the farther door seen in the photograph; the door in the foreground leads into the stable above which is a storage loft.

A Derbyshire farm typical of the continuous linear layout found in this region; derivative, probably, from the longhouse but without interior communication between the house and the other parts which can include not merely barn, byre and hay-store, but also granary, wagon sheds and stables.

◀

Bickleigh Mill Farm, Devon; typical of the rather haphazard layout of a great many farms. The buildings vary a great deal in date and are quite separate from the farmhouse, a case of gradual organic growth as new needs arose.

Gressenhall; a Norfolk farm in the chalk and flint area. A compact linear arrangement but with the house separated from the farm buildings.

▶

early and deeply rooted traditions in layout as well as in the construction of certain types of farm buildings, particularly barns and granaries. There are farmsteads in which both the accommodation for livestock and storage of crops are attached directly to the farmhouse. In this category the simplest and probably the oldest in terms of ancestry is usually described as a 'longhouse' – already referred to on page 54 – in which the accommodation of cattle is continuous with

and accessible to the lower end of the hall under one continuous roof. In such buildings storage for hay was often also provided in a loft above the byre. There can, however, be considerable variations of this basic plan. The hall can be directly open to the byre, with one door providing access to both byres and hall, with perhaps a step from the hall floor down to that of the byres and a partial screen; or there can be a more complete separation but still with a door leading

71

directly from house part to byre. From this very close integration, which for the sake of classification has been given the name 'longhouse', there can be many stages before we arrive at complete separation and isolation of farmhouse from farm buildings. There can be one roof but independent access to farm buildings set at right-angles but joined to the house part, or arranged to form three sides of a courtyard plan, or a completely closed courtyard. The latter was the plan usually adopted for the many 'model' farms in the late eighteenth and early nineteenth centuries. All these forms of co-ordination can be found in most regions, but certain of them are restricted to fairly well-defined areas. The longhouse may be found in the South and West, but more frequently on the upland than in the lowland; the laithe-house is to be seen mainly in Yorkshire. The various forms of courtyard plan exist almost everywhere except in the East and South-East, where the physical attachment of farm buildings of any kind to the house is exceedingly rare. There the pattern of layout is more haphazard and varies greatly from area to area.

Barns

Of the two principal classes of farm-building – those to accommodate livestock and those for storage – it is the storage barns for the corn harvest which are usually of the greatest interest. In corn-growing areas barns needed to be large enough to store the whole grain crop at harvest time. This was then gradually threshed on the threshing floor between the two opposing doors, in the winter. These barns were commonly the largest buildings on the farmstead, and those built on the great monastic estates were among the finest structures of the Middle Ages. They not only represent the carpenters' craft in its simplest and purest form, but also, because the whole structure is exposed, they can be studied in a way that is not possible in any other kind of building. William Morris considered the great Cistercian barn at Great Coxwell (see page 31) the most beautiful building in England, and one can understand what he meant. Freed from the often conflicting considerations of complex interior plans or adornment the carpenter was able to concentrate on what

Bredon barn, Worcestershire; a tithe barn of the fourteenth century. The room with the chimney above the second porch can be paralleled by other examples where some domestic accommodation has been provided in barns.

would secure maximum strength and stability with the minimum wastage of costly principal timber. Bay divisions could be planned with these considerations only in mind. Except for door openings which had to be wide and high enough to allow loaded wagons to be drawn inside and unloaded and then, without turning, to emerge through doors on the opposite side, there was no interior plan to be considered except that of eliminating, where practicable, the tie-beam in order to give greater head-room for unloading and stacking. The distance bays were apart therefore depended on the overall size of the barn and strength of the timber framework, and in practice was of a fairly constant measurement, usually between ten and twelve feet. In some smaller barns with slighter timber framing the entrance bay may be found to be a little wider than the other bays. Correspondingly, in the larger and more massively constructed barns, it may be slightly less, or have the difference taken up by the addition of separate doorposts within the bay division.

It has been suggested that bay division measurements originated from, or are at least related to, the standard Saxon unit of land measurement – the five and a half yards of the 'rod, pole or perch', and that this was also the measurement required to accommodate the stalls for a plough team of four oxen. If there was originally any such connection, it is clear that the bay measurements of medieval and later buildings had long ceased to have any such connection. It is true that when, in the thirteenth century, the site for a new town such as Winchelsea was laid out with streets and building plots, the measurements were all multiples of the standard rod, pole or perch. This may have affected the general size and planning of the buildings, but there seems to be absolutely no evidence that it had any direct relationship to the measurements of interior structural divisions.

Barns reflect in a simplified, easily accessible form, the traditions prevailing in each area at the time of building. Where a simple unaisled barn is contemporary with a farmhouse in a timber building area, the skeleton of each, if they could be seen together, omitting the partitions and linings from the house, would often be almost indistinguishable. A few details of barns have already been used to illustrate differences of roof structure, but each area has its own variations and characteristic forms. Because of their size they mirror magnificently in their roof cladding and walls the qualities of the local landscape; but one reserva-

tion should be made. During the last hundred and fifty years the cladding of timber-built barns and other farm buildings with tarred or creosoted sawn soft-wood weatherboard has been almost universal. This is certainly not how most of those built before the eighteenth century would have been covered. Some, as we have seen, may

Small aisled barn re-erected at the Weald and Downland Museum. In this plan the aisles are taken round the ends. This seems to be a form only found in the South-East, and to date from the seventeenth century. A photograph taken during re-erection is on page 29.

never have had anything more than unplastered woven wattle infill between timber frames; others would have had standard wattle and daub. In the seventeenth century many had brick infill, and a few survive with panels of stone or flint. Granaries in particular under later weatherboard exteriors frequently preserve brick or wattle and daub panels. Where weatherboarding was used — and a good deal still survives — it seems usually to have been of wide oak boards untreated. In some areas in the South-East, barns built in the sixteenth and seventeenth centuries have been found with the upper half infilled with wattle and daub and the lower half covered with original oak weatherboarding. This treatment of barns is closely analogous to the application of tile hanging and weatherboarding to houses.

Barns are the least protected and the most vulnerable of our larger traditional buildings. Occasionally one may be converted to other uses, and a few outstanding ones are pre-

Brook; an aisled barn maintained as an agricultural museum by Wye College, similar in size to the Bredon barn, but timber-framed.

served as important buildings in their own right. Relatively few have any role in modern life. They are costly to repair and through neglect may become dangerous. Judging from the region I know best, I would say that at least one barn each week is destroyed without trace, and often without record, over the country as a whole.

Hay Barns and Cattle Sheds

Similar types of farming may lead to similar solutions in widely separated areas. For example, in predominantly dairy-farming regions of the Midlands and the South-East, the building of byres attached to hay barns at some distance from the rest of the farmsteads is common to both; but whereas in the South-East the byre and barns are large, and often include an enclosed yard, in the uplands of the Pennines they are small and more closely integrated, the storage barn being little more than a hayloft above a couple of cattle stalls. The 'linhay' in areas of Devon is another solution, but is usually more closely related to the rest of the farm buildings. Today these outlying barns and byres are rapidly becoming derelict since they meet the requirements neither of modern methods of milking nor of hygiene.

Another combination of uses is the 'bank barn' found in a limited area in Cumbria – with the storage of grain above and cattle at a lower level. The threshed straw provided bedding for the cattle below. These barns were necessarily built on a slope, providing easy access by cart at the higher level and drainage for the byre at the lower level, and were conditioned by the hilly nature of the locality. But similar conditions exist in many other parts of the country and barns of this sort are found, but are exceptional. Perhaps 80 to 90 per cent of all barns recorded of this type are situated in this one rather circumscribed area. This leaves the question unanswered as to why there rather than elsewhere; one would not be justified in assuming that this form was first evolved and developed in that area; and the same kind of question applies to many other established local traditions.

Granaries

Next to the barn the most important storage building was the granary, i.e. where grain was stored after threshing. Sometimes grain seems to have been stored on an upper floor within the barn, or even in the farmhouse itself, but well before the end of the Middle Ages it was usual on the larger farms to build separate granaries providing greater protection from vermin and damp. These were raised from the ground on piers or walls, providing a space for carts or other stores underneath. The use of mushroom-shaped

'Bank barn' – typical of parts of Cumbria.

Granary built with a storage shed at Cogge's Manor Farm Museum, Oxfordshire.

Two granaries re-erected at Lackham Agricultural College, Wiltshire, forming part of an agricultural museum. One is of two storeys, on fifteen mushroom-shaped staddle-stones, the other is of the more standard type (on nine staddles), an exact square, and typical of the South-East.

Granary of two storeys at Eastergate in Sussex, restored and adapted to serve as a parish room. The very regular round staddle-stones – as compared with the roughly hewn stones of the Lackham granaries – were, in the eighteenth and early nineteenth centuries being mass-produced in quarries at Portland and in the Isle of Wight, and were shipped to all parts of the South-East. By the middle of the nineteenth century cast-iron mushroom-shaped supports were being cast in Birmingham and other centres and distributed all over the country for both granaries and hay-stacks.

'staddle' stones, which seems to be limited mainly to the Southern and Eastern parts of England, appears to date to the Tudor period and to have become customary by the early eighteenth century.

Like the barns, granaries vary enormously in size, shape, and in the materials with which they were built. They may be long and narrow, or exact squares, and of one or two storeys, while their roof structures and roof covering reflect the traditions of each locality as closely as do those of the farmhouses and other farm buildings.

One difficulty in interpreting and understanding our traditional building heritage is that all such buildings were designed to meet the needs of a particular society at a particular time. These needs have been continually changing; but what does strike anyone looking at almost any group of farm buildings is that, if we ignore the additions and alterations of the last hundred years or so, we are usually left with a group of buildings which harmonise, however varied in date, quite surprisingly well with their surroundings. At the time they were built they were also perfectly fitted to fulfil the functions for which they were designed. It is these build-

Granary at Avoncroft Museum with open wagon shed below. A form general south of the Trent.

75

ings on most farms that are usually neglected, in decay, or already ruinous.

Water- and Wind-Mills

Another building which served an essential need of the agricultural community was the mill. Both the water-powered mill and the windmill have a special attraction, particularly when they can be seen working. The watermill preceded the windmill and ground most of the corn in the Middle Ages. Several thousand watermills are recorded in Domesday Survey. These were probably all fairly small; by the seventeenth century there were not only many more, but most of them were much larger, and although surviving mills are often built on sites recorded in Domesday, few of the actual structures date back beyond the seventeenth century. The casualty list, since the coming of other forms of power in the nineteenth century, has probably been greater than that for any other type of building connected with agriculture. In most counties efforts have been made since the war to preserve and restore one or two representative examples, and four have been dismantled and re-erected as exhibits in open air museums (see Singleton, page 47 and Stowmarket, page 118).

Horizontal mill reconstructed at Shawbost in the Hebrides. In this type of mill – also called 'Norse' – the waterwheel has no rim and the blades revolve horizontally. Many of the watermills listed in Domesday Survey in the north of England (or wherever there was a sufficiently rapid stream) may have been of this type. A much slower stream, but with a greater quantity of flow was all that was needed to drive an overshot mill where the weight of water caught in 'buckets' on the wheel gives the power.

Overshot mill re-erected at St Fagans Museum.

Detail of blades of the horizontal mill at Shawbost.

Tide Mill, Woodbridge, Essex. Well-restored and open to the public; this type of watermill was once fairly widespread in the estuaries of the South-East. Its main drawback was that it could only be used for two or three hours in any twenty-four when sufficient head of water had been penned in the upper storage pond at high tide to drive the wheel when the tide receded.

The windmill is relatively a newcomer. The first windmills seem to have been introduced in the thirteenth or late twelfth century, probably by crusaders returning from the eastern Mediterranean where they had been in use for centuries. At first regarded as an unreliable and unpredictable novelty, they became by the sixteenth century, with the growth of population, a valuable additional source of power; by then water was already over-exploited and there was continual conflict over its use.

The hey-day of the windmill was between the middle of the eighteenth and nineteenth centuries, by which time steam power became available. Like the early watermills, the earliest windmills were small, and up to the eighteenth century were post-mills. In these the whole structure was pivoted on a central post to enable it to be turned into the

Cross in Hand, post-mill, Sussex; this is a type of late post-mill in which the whole mill is turned automatically by the tail shaft being attached to a fantail and to a cogged 'roundabout' fixed to the ground round the mill.

wind by a hand-propelled shaft. In the eighteenth century the 'smock' and 'tower' mills were introduced in which the only part that turned was the cap containing the sails and the driving shaft. The smock mill was timber-framed and usually eight-sided, the tower mill was stone- or brick-built and normally round. By the nineteenth century virtually all mills being built were of these two last types. Technological advances, most of which were introduced from Holland, took the windmill right outside the category of traditional and vernacular. Relatively few of the earlier post-mills now survive, and the majority of windmills which have been preserved in one way or another, sometimes by conversion to dwellings, are tower or smock mills – though often these have lost their sails. A hundred years ago there were few places in the corn-growing lowland areas of England which were not within sight of at least one or two windmills. Conservation and restoration of what remain have been taken more seriously since the war, and in most counties in East Anglia and the South-East two or three have been preserved representing characteristic forms – some by Local Authorities, some by Preservation Societies and Trusts.

Shipley smock mill, Sussex; this photograph of the head of the smock mill illustrates the movable cap which holds the shaft and sails and which is turned into the wind by very elaborate gearing between the fan-tail and the cogged, circular plate on which the head revolves.

Windmills, however, embody local traditions and relate to the landscape less than watermills, which preserve a variety in structure and design far exceeding the relatively standardised form of the windmill.

Wind and water were not only harnessed to corn grinding; they were often applied to other uses. For example, wind-power was used to pump water, and in the Fens there were said to be several thousand windpumps in the seven-

West Blatchington, near Brighton; a windmill built on the roof of a barn to work agricultural machinery inside the barn.

teenth century, only one of which survives, preserved by the National Trust on Wicken Fen. One that was used to pump water on the Pevensey Level in Sussex has been reconstructed at the Weald and Downland Museum.

Windpump from the Pevensey Levels for raising water, re-erected at the Weald and Downland Museum.

Horse Gins and Round Houses

Another source of power was the horse or the ox. The employment of animals was by means of a 'roundabout' in which the horse, donkey or ox walked a circular track

Early nineteenth-century round house (on the left of the photograph) attached to barn re-erected at the Ryedale Open Air Museum.

harnessed in such a way that a central shaft was turned which transmitted by cog-wheels or pulleys power to various kinds of machinery. It was much used for lifting weights by ropes passing over pulleys, particularly for raising water from wells. These roundabouts usually involved the erection of buildings to provide shelter and protect the machinery. These structures are called round houses, though frequently they were octagonal or even twelve-sided. This roundabout device was also used for crushing materials such as apples for cider-making or bark for tanning. Their multiplication and rapid decline followed the same pattern as in the case of windmills. The few that survive are mostly late buildings, and attached to the outside of barns with shafts connecting to the increasingly complex machinery inside the barns ranging from chaff cutters to threshing machines.

A vertical form of the same principle is the treadwheel worked by donkeys or humans, and sometimes illustrated in medieval manuscript drawings. These were particularly used as lifting devices bringing up water from wells, goods

Vertical treadwheel, probably early seventeenth century, for raising water from a deep well, re-erected at the Weald and Downland Museum.

at wharves or heavy building material, over pulleys, at great heights in the construction of tall buildings such as castles and churches. One for raising water and dating, probably, from the early seventeenth century, has been re-erected at the Weald and Downland Museum.

Dovecotes

Another kind of round house (occasionally square) serving a very different kind of purpose, and anathema to the peasant, but very widespread in the Middle Ages and up to the nineteenth century, was the dovecote. Up to the sixteenth century these were associated with manor houses or monasteries, but a surprising number of small dovecotes were built in the eighteenth century by prosperous yeomen farmers – perhaps to assert status. Pigeon pie was not only a delicacy; pigeons formed a fairly important source of food supply, but whether it was good economy, considering the grain the birds consumed, is another matter. The largest dovecote we have record of is the one built by the great Cluniac priory of St Pancras, near Lewes. This still stood in the eighteenth century, though nothing survives above ground today. It was in the form of a great cross with four roughly square towers and is reckoned to have contained nesting recesses for nearly three thousand birds. An average-sized dovecote would contain probably some five to six hundred compartments. One which still retains its 'potence', (a ladder attached to a central revolving perpendicular shaft, to enable easy access to the nesting recesses), is open to the public at Dunster in Somerset. Many less complete, and often ruinous, survive in most counties dating from every century from the fifteenth to the nineteenth.

Ruined circular dovecote, possibly fourteenth century, in the grounds of The White House Museum, Shropshire. Some of the nesting boxes are exposed; they cover completely the interior wall space.

Barn with nesting boxes (dovecote) above covered entry at Kelmscott in the Cotswolds.

An eighteenth-century oast house now part of the Agricultural Museum at Brook.

Recommended Further Reading

NIGEL HARVEY, *History of Farm Buildings*.
NIGEL HARVEY, *Old Farm Buildings*.
    In the 'Shire' series, a short, attractively produced booklet.
COOK & SMITH, *English Farmhouses and Cottages*.
    A finely illustrated picture book.
W.G. HOSKINS, *History from the Farm*.
    Accounts of the development of a number of farms in various parts of the British Isles.
R. WAILES, *Windmills of England: a study of their origin, development and future*.
L. SYSON, *British Watermills*.
    A comprehensive survey.
A.B. COOKE, *A Book of Dovecotes*.

Public and Communal Buildings

Buildings belonging to the community or serving some communal use have a special fascination. By their nature they are more accessible and a fair number have been little altered since they were built. They range from bridges and market halls to shops and hospitals. Although much has been lost they still form an exceedingly rich heritage and reflect the varied pattern of traditional building perhaps more completely than does any other category. It is not easy to decide what falls within the vernacular and the transition from the small brotherhood hall or parish room to the great guild-

Packhorse bridge at Allerford, north-west Somerset, now under the protection of the Department for the Environment. The bridge, houses and cobbled road are all in harmony through the consistent use of local stone. A few hundred yards upstream the mill has been restored by local enthusiasts.

The courthouse at Long Crendon, Bedfordshire. This building is owned by the National Trust. The hall of four bays is open to the public. The ground floor is divided into separate cottages and access to the Upper Hall is by a stair in the fifth (end) bay. The front facing the road is jettied.

halls, or from the simple market halls to the grand buildings which once graced the centres of many of our cities is a gradual one, and the line between vernacular and 'polite' not easy to draw.

We still use the simple clapper bridges of Dartmoor and a few surviving packhorse bridges of the upland regions, while some magnificent bridges of the fourteenth and fifteenth centuries stand up to the weight of modern transport. It is the smaller, more truly vernacular examples which have suffered most destruction – such as the packhorse bridges once general in those parts of the country where transport was virtually impossible for wheeled vehicles.

Market and Guild Halls

Although the church provided accommodation for public meetings and communal uses of various kinds, the manor-house also often included a room which could serve as a courtroom. These were usually situated at one end of the hall at first-floor level and had an external stair. Evidence for these exists from the thirteenth century onwards, and it is possibly because of this tradition that later halls from the fifteenth to the seventeenth centuries built specifically for some

communal use were often designed at first-floor level over an open arcade or undercroft, the latter meeting some other need as stores, stables, or workshops. Such upper halls tend to be long and narrow. The fifteenth-century brotherhood hall at Steyning (later to become the Grammar School), consists of seven bays and is jettied on the side facing the street. The Wool Hall at Newbury is of five bays, the court-houses and guildhalls at Long Crendon, Elstow and Finchingfield are all of four bays, and this would seem to be the most favoured kind of plan and proportion. These halls are usually situated in the main street or market place, often over an open arcaded ground storey. At the open air museum at Singleton two such upper halls have been re-erected. One is a typical small free-standing market hall over an open arcade, and jettied on both sides. The other, longer and narrower, is jettied only on one side. They represent in their different plans and proportions the two main styles. All these examples are timber built. In stone areas, except for the jettying, plans were similar.

The purposes that these first-floor halls served were varied. At Leicester the sixteenth-century grammar school is actually built in the market place over an open arcade. At Faversham the plan of the grammar school situated at the edge of the town is very like the centrally sited market hall.

'The Church House', Crowcombe, Somerset. This upper hall now serves as the Parish room. The stone access stair is built against the end of the building.

Another type of building associated with market towns and one which probably has a very early history (although there are few surviving examples which can take us back beyond the fifteenth century) is the 'butter' or market cross. Such buildings were no doubt built on a site previously occupied by a simple cross raised on a series of steps marking the centre of the market, an interesting example being that at Castle Coombe in Wiltshire. These one-storey, open-arcaded structures served the needs of the market. They were often richly decorated with picturesque and elaborate roofs.

Hospitals and almshouses form another large category of buildings, and range from simple vernacular to buildings on the grandest scale such as the early fourteenth-century hospital or Maison Dieu at Dover that still survives in part. The word 'hospital' is from the same root as hostel, and in the Middle Ages there was no clear distinction between the inn serving the individual traveller's or pilgrim's needs, and the complex foundations meeting some more specific requirement, such as the care of the sick and the aged. Most towns of any size contained at least one building endowed and designed mainly for the care of the sick, the old and infirm, as distinct from the traveller or pilgrim. These were normally organised on a semi-religious basis, and followed a modified monastic rule. The only clear distinction in our

A late medieval building at Great Chart, Kent, traditionally known as the 'Pest House'. From the twelfth century onwards, dwellings and even small hamlets were built on the outskirts of towns and some villages for the accommodation of lepers. This is at the edge of the churchyard and may be a rare survival of such a building.

modern sense was in the case of leper houses or colonies, which were invariably situated well outside the town.

The medieval hospital had two main forms – the courtyard plan, very similar in layout to that of an Oxford college, bearing certain similarities to the regular monastic cloister plan, and the other, that of a single building under one continuous roof in which accommodation for the occupants was provided on both sides of a wide central nave leading to a chapel and an altar that all could see. Because many of these medieval all-purpose 'hospitals' were administered by the monasteries most were destroyed when the latter were dissolved. A few were taken over by the civic authorities, but the majority fell into ruin, and part of the needs they had met were supplied in the later sixteenth and in the seventeenth centuries by new secular foundations – particularly in the case of almshouses for the old and infirm.

These later foundations have been luckier in their survival, and although not quite adapted to modern standards many are still cared for and occupied. There are, in fact, few towns of any historic significance which do not possess at least one example and in some relatively small towns, such as Petworth in Sussex or Abingdon in Berkshire, there were as many as three or four such foundations. These endowments date mostly from the period when brick was being used over the whole lowland area wherever good brick-making clays were found. They demonstrate perhaps better than any other class of building how local traditions in the use of brick were already becoming established, and they did much to help establish such traditions.

Inns and Ale Houses

Ale-houses and shops form another class of buildings designed for public use or public service. Up to the nineteenth century ale-houses in towns were far more numerous than inns. Where records survive from the seventeenth or eighteenth centuries one is surprised by their numbers. They were far less permanent than the inns, not being specifically built for the purpose, being more often than not adaptations of shops or houses.

Inns provided food and accommodation, and a fair

St Mary's Almshouse, Glastonbury. Built in the four-teenth century as two terraces facing each other across a narrow alley, they represent an early example of a very humble terrace, and can be compared with the later, much more elaborate terrace treatment in the Vicars Close in the neighbouring city of Wells (page 64). The terrace on one side has been demolished.

The John Smith Almshouses (1657) Canterbury; these terraced almshouses in brick illustrate the Dutch influence in the South-East, and the ornamental use of brick.

'The George', a typical courtyard inn at Burford (Oxfordshire).

number can claim, quite correctly, to have existed before the sixteenth century. Surviving examples suggest that the traditional form was that of a courtyard open at one end or entirely enclosed with an entrance large enough for the passage of wagons, with space in the courtyard for these, in or under which many would spend the night. We must remember, however, that up to the sixteenth century a good deal of travelling was made possible and relatively easy for the poorer classes by the provision of pilgrims' hostels, so that the increase in the number of inns, as also of almshouses, is essentially a feature of the sixteenth and seventeenth centuries, and linked with the dissolution of the monasteries. It may, however, be a mistake to imagine that the average person in the Middle Ages was less mobile, or travelled less, than his or her counterpart in the seventeenth or even the eighteenth centuries, but unfortunately conclusive evidence is lacking. The ale-house and the inn can be said to

correspond up to a point to the public house and the hotel of today.

Shops

Like the word hospital, the idea of a shop has changed its meaning considerably within the last hundred and fifty years. Before that time most shops were simply 'work' shops with a counter to display the goods being produced. The list of tradesmen in any town or village in the seventeenth or eighteenth centuries is virtually a list of the workers producing different kinds of basic goods — cordwainers (footwear), bakers, tailors and so on. The goods were mostly made on the premises; today shops are 99 per cent merely retailing centres for goods produced elsewhere. The saddler or clockmaker, working in a room behind the counter, still existed in many villages fifty years ago, but rarely today. Up to the eighteenth century most

Shop front with surviving shutters at Lavenham (Suffolk). This late medieval shop front preserves everything but the counter, which would probably have projected over the pavement. It forms part of the National Trust property which includes the magnificently decorated timber-framed Guildhall.

Reconstruction drawing of a late medieval shop and street in Horsham (Sussex). Most of the structure of the shop still survived behind the later nineteenth- or early twentieth-century facade. It was discovered during demolition, salvaged, and is to be re-erected at the Weald and Downland Open Air Museum (see page 39). There is evidence for all the buildings depicted in this drawing. Most of them still exist behind later facades and alterations.

shops were open-fronted, and work was done behind lattices or shutters which could be partly closed in cold or windy weather. Of all our traditional building forms the old-style shop is the one which has most completely disappeared, and the only possibility of seeing what was meant by a shop before the nineteenth century will be through reconstructions in museums.

Reconstructions of shop frontages and their immediate interiors as they existed in the nineteenth century have been made at the London Museum, at the Castle Museum in York (page 126), the Salford Museum, the Kirkstall Museum near Leeds, and on a more limited scale in a number of other museums. All these are furnished as they might have been about a century or so ago. In Coventry (page 99) a number of timber-framed shops which survived the bombing are being moved from other areas and re-erected in one street – Spon Street. Some of these date back to the fifteenth and sixteenth centuries, and as far as is practicable they are being adapted to present-day use. They are accessible as far as the ground floor, but since they must fit into modern commercial usage they give little idea of what a typical shop of any period before the eighteenth century would have looked like.

Smithies and Wheelwrights' Shops

Of buildings connected with a craft or trade the smithy and the wheelwright's shop were as essential to most communities as the mill. We know from early manuscripts that the basic elements – hearth, tools, bellows, etc. – changed very little in design from Norman times to the twentieth century. What we do not know is how far the buildings themselves have altered: probably not a great deal in plan or size, but very few that survive can be dated back beyond the seventeenth century. The majority of those still functioning date from the eighteenth and nineteenth centuries, and these are rapidly disappearing or being converted to other uses. Tanyards, which have almost entirely disappeared within the last fifty years, were once numerous; most market towns and some villages had a tanyard on their outskirts. At the

Smithy and Wheelwright's shop. This is one of the buildings salvaged and re-erected in the Open Air Museum at St Fagans. As was frequently the case, the crafts of smith and wheelwright were combined and carried out in one building.

Tanyard complex re-erected at St Fagans Open Air Museum.

open air museum at St Fagans a rather larger than average example has been meticulously reconstructed.

Warehouses

Warehouses and storage buildings comprise another group. A few are left which can take us back to the Middle Ages, such as the Norman warehouse known as 'The Marlipins' at Shoreham in Sussex (see page 90), the recently restored 'Town Cellars' at Poole in Dorset, or the storeyed and jettied examples at King's Lynn, one of which is called the 'Hanseatic Warehouse'. Merchants' houses were also often built over underground storage vaults. After the air raids on Southampton several such cellars were found beneath the rubble of collapsed buildings of much later date. Similar cellars or undercrofts have also been found recently at Winchelsea, dating from the late thirteenth century.

Toll Cottages

Mention has already been made of the thousands of toll cottages built mostly between 1750 and 1810 for the network

Warehouses at Totnes (Devon). The earliest of these probably dates from the seventeenth century and is built entirely of local stone and tiled. Warehouses represent, perhaps, the simplest form of purpose-built structures, devoid of ornamentation but integrating with the landscape (see also 'The Marlipins', page 90, where a decorated façade was added to an earlier Norman building in the thirteenth century.

A toll cottage re-erected at the Ironbridge Gorge Museum, Shropshire. The stone tiles provide a tenuous link with local tradition.

A typical mid-nineteenth-century Church School and head-teacher's house: very self-conscious 'Jacobethan' style but using local materials.

of Turnpike Trusts which were transforming road communications over the whole country. These were designed within the generally accepted Georgian vocabulary, but using local materials and conforming to local traditions so far as was practicable. At this period continuity of style was up to a point assumed and this lasted until the cult of the 'cottage ornée' and the 'picturesque' introduced an entirely novel element which had little if any relation to tradition or locality.

Schools

It is interesting to compare the simple toll cottages with the thousands of church and state schools built a couple of generations later in virtually every village in the country. These were usually quite small, and in plan were a kind of junior version of the smaller Grammar Schools of an earlier tradition, very often consisting of one large hall with a headmaster's house adjacent. There was clearly an attempt on the part of the architects responsible to try to relate their designs and the use of materials to the locality, although the

resultant buildings were usually marred by the adoption of a neo-Gothic archaic manner, plus the usual heavy-handed and over-emphatic decoration typical of the Victorian period. They do, however, present the very real dilemma facing any architect concerned about the disintegration of local forms, whether he is designing a new house on the edge of a Cotswold village or in a Lakeland valley. The designers of Victorian village schools often took great care in the selection and use of appropriate local material, but failed when faced with the problem of recreating traditions in design which had already disintegrated.

Recommended Further Reading

Very few studies, apart from rather specialised monographs, are available about the many forms of traditional building touched on in this chapter, but *The English Almshouse with some account of its predecessors, the medieval hospital* by Walter Godfrey can be strongly recommended. It illustrates the great variety in plan and design which could be achieved within the framework of a generally accepted tradition.

Adaptation to Needs; and the Decay of Tradition

The older a building the more it is liable to be altered and adapted to changing needs or fashions. This is particularly true of houses and cottages, and especially of those built of timber. In these it is relatively easy to build out under jetties, to change partitions, insert floors, and alter completely door and window openings. It is also the smaller houses rather than the greater mansions which are easiest to transform.

In the regions where stone, cob or brick dominate there is much less remodelling, and it is much easier to recognise what there is. Straight joints in brickwork or masonry reveal immediately, even to the unpractised eye, where additions have been made, or windows or door openings sealed up, or roof lines changed. Farm buildings also are less drastically modified, and because their skeletal structure is more visible, alterations, additions or rebuilding can much more readily be detected. This chapter will be mainly concerned with

The Marlipins, Shoreham, Sussex. An interesting example of refacing in the Middle Ages. The basic structure is twelfth century, and Norman; a century later the end fronting the street was given a facelift in the new Gothic manner in the form of a chequerboard skin of alternate squares of light Caen stone and knapped flint. It seems to have been built to serve as a warehouse and like the later medieval (recently restored) 'town cellars' at Poole, it now houses a museum. The timber roof is not original but the unusual arcaded undercroft probably is.

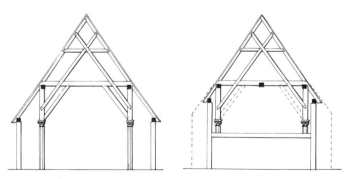

Diagram showing how an aisled hall was converted into a hall without aisles. When the aisle posts were removed the central space or 'nave' was increased by underpinning the sawn-off aisle posts with a longer and more massive supporting beam inserted underneath.

These two jettied buildings each now consisting of three cottages may at first sight appear similar in construction and probably sixteenth century in date. In fact, the one on the left started life at least a century earlier than the one on the right, as a 'Wealden' house with a recessed central open hall. (See page 40.)

illustrations of a few of the many ways in which timber houses have been modified and their appearance so altered that only during reconstruction or demolition have some been recognised. We have mentioned how, before the end of the Middle Ages, aisles were not infrequently removed, but it is during the sixteenth and seventeenth centuries in the period of transition from open hearth to chimney, that reconstruction became general, and few domestic buildings except those in the remotest areas escaped some alteration. An examination of the roofs of houses built in the Middle Ages will often reveal a succession of modifications (as described on pages 57–8), culminating in the insertion of chimney breasts built on such a scale that it was possible to sit on either side within the inglenook round a fire which retained some resemblance to the old unenclosed hearth. These changes in plan are often so concealed today, and the principles of construction remain so consistent, that it may be quite impossible, except for evidence of sooting in the roof timbers, to determine whether a timber-framed house with a central chimney breast was built in the late Tudor or early Stuart period, or very much earlier as a medieval open hall converted later to the new style of living.

The substitution of these massive chimney breasts for open hearths, although drastically altering the interior plan, did not necessarily affect the external appearance except for the chimney heads which now superseded the medieval louvres or where massive chimneys were built against the side or end of houses. It is rather later that the exteriors began to be so

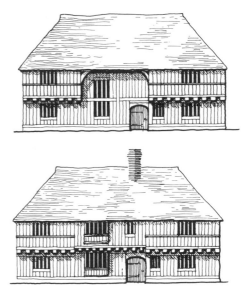

This diagram illustrates how easily the alteration from a Wealden to a continuous jettied house could be made when the open hearth was given up and joists to carry a floor inserted.

A Wealden at Steyning divided into two independent tenements, and right, a reconstruction of this house as originally built.

The final stage in the modification of a Wealden house. In this example, judging from the different treatments and materials, it seems to have been very much a step-by-step process.

completely transformed that from any external view it may be impossible to identify the original structure and decide in what century it may have been built. The feature which particularly lends itself to alteration is the jetty. There are various ways in which this could be modified to fit changing ideas. We can see this particularly clearly in the case of

the 'Wealden' type of house. To convert these into continuous jettied houses – when the latter in the sixteenth century became fashionable – was done by the simple expedient of joining up the jetties on each side of the hall when the latter was divided horizontally and joists inserted to carry the new floor at first-floor level. The next phase took place when the continuous jetty fell out of favour. The aim then was to extend the size of the ground floor, which could be done by pushing the wall out to the edge of the jetty, thus eliminating the jetty altogether and at the same time taking in a slice of the public highway. The results of this second phase of the transformation are often surprising. Usually the original timber frame which supported the jetty was replaced on the new line by brick, but it might be by stone, and occasionally by re-using the original posts. There is, then, little relationship between this underpinning of the jetty and what is left above. Structural changes usually ended at this point, but not the surface treatment; part or entire tile-hanging, weather-boarding, or simple plastering in the eighteenth and nineteenth centuries could carry further the transformation. Disguises can be so complete that 'Wealden' houses are still being found hidden under these later 'improvements'. Confusion is often made greater by the

Front elevation of 'Detillens' at Limpsfield in Surrey and a side view showing how a timber house with its roof may be completely freestanding behind brick Georgian façades. In this case there is little relationship between the windows and doors in the Georgian façade and those of the original house. What may be found more surprising in this example is that the original house was in fact a Wealden, with jettied bays on each side of the hall, and these have been cut off. The interior of the hall roof is accessible and its structure exposed.

The photograph and drawing of the end of the façade shows how the original jetty was cut off and replaced by the Georgian brick façade.

splitting up of these large houses into two or even three small cottages, involving equally drastic alteration of the interior.

What happened to so many 'Wealden' houses, happened to other jettied buildings, but without the need to bring forward the recessed hall wall at first-floor level.

These are a few examples of structural alterations to meet changed concepts of plan. From the eighteenth century onwards alterations have been less structurally drastic, but often equally effective in hiding those parts of a building visible in village street or town. In the case of timber building it took many different forms, one being the addition of an outer skin of brickwork often quite independent of the load-bearing timber structure behind. Later, in the Regency period, the application of stucco plaster, sometimes grooved to create an illusion of masonry, became very general, and there seems to have been a revulsion from timber which was generally down-graded in esteem. We have already referred to the ingenious form of tile-hanging which simulated brickwork, known as 'mathematical tiling'. The widespread use of this in the South-East was probably stimulated by the imposition of a tax on bricks; it is strange that it was not equally popular in other parts of the country. It was not

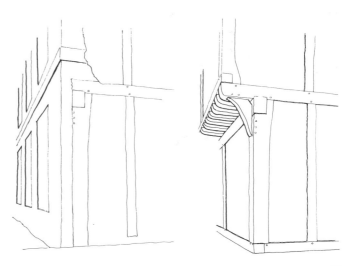

Three-storeyed town house in Midhurst, Sussex, built probably between 1540 and 1560. Up to the present century it was one of a series of such houses adjacent to each other. At the end of the last war it was saved from demolition and these photographs illustrate the stages before, during and after restoration. Apart from the complete plastering over and concealment of the decorative timber-framing, the structure had been little altered, and in the main room at first-floor level some remarkably well preserved wall paintings were found underneath layers of later plaster and wallpaper.

limited to timber and can be found on the façade side of flint buildings. The use of stucco or painted plaster seems also to have spread from the South-East when Brighton was possibly the most fashionable centre in the country (roughly from 1790 to 1830) and where it was used to cover brick, stone, flint and timber concealing everything which relates a building to its natural environment.

As well as exteriors, interiors also can have their character considerably modified by surface treatment without any change of plan or structure. It was in the period of transition and rebuilding during the sixteenth and seventeenth centuries that the development of interior decoration could create a real difference in the quality and atmosphere of interior space, even though dimensions and proportions remained unaltered. The most obvious of these alterations in surface

treatment was the increase in the use of wood panelling. Panelling was nothing new, but whereas medieval panelling was usually massive and integral with the structure, sixteenth- and seventeenth-century panelling was applied as a kind of veneer, and the tendency throughout the period was to reduce its substance while increasing the fineness and sophistication of the mouldings. The earliest forms were designed to conceal vertical jointing, the later forms to create small rectangular panels. There is, however, a question as to whether darkening has been increased by centuries of polishing; in the seventeenth century much panelling may have been lighter, and in many cases it seems to have been painted – sometimes in bright primary colours on a lighter background. Panelling of this kind was expensive, and rarely reached down to the vernacular level, but there is

94

Wattle and daub panel in a medieval hall with combed decoration darkened with soot, revealed under a coat of later plaster.

Late sixteenth-century decoration on a plastered wattle and daub panel found under later reed plaster laid on laths, which fortunately protected the mural paintings. Both examples on this page can now be seen in the Weald and Downland Museum.

growing evidence for a very great increase in painted decoration which did spread to this level, particularly in the South-East. In the Middle Ages the traditional form of wall decoration in timber buildings was that of simple combed designs on the surface of the wattle and daub infill. This was very often covered in the sixteenth century with a smooth lime plaster on which was stencilled (or painted freehand) ornamental designs, usually black on white base, but sometimes polychrome. Occasionally these painted decorations simulate panelling.

Another development before the end of the sixteenth century was the printing of wallpaper in small rectangular sheets, usually with heraldic designs – shields, heraldic animals, etc. Such decoration is continually coming to light through greater interest and care in examining what may lie hidden under later plaster, wallpaper and paint; it may often

have supplemented or replaced 'hanging cloths' which are sometimes mentioned in early inventories, a kind of 'poor man's tapestry'.

Returning to the exterior, another very general alteration, and one which could be equally destructive of external features, was the addition of outshots, in which the roof was continued downwards to form an extension at the side or ends, or both, of a dwelling. Such additions change, and often ruin, the original proportions of a building. This is true also of relatively minor alterations such as the size, positioning and form of windows and doors. The introduction of sash windows from the end of the seventeenth century onwards, replacing earlier casements, was often accompanied by such alterations. More perplexing can be the alteration of the height of roofs by raising walls, and the addition of dormer windows, or by the building of completely independent skin walls to a height above the original eaves level and with a parapet hiding the original roof. There is another form of alteration that does not hinge so much on the individual building as on its relationship to its

Pendean farmhouse re-erected at the Weald and Downland Open Air Museum; built towards the end of the sixteenth century as a small farmhouse it was later divided into two cottages and outshots were added at various times which eventually enclosed and concealed three-quarters of the building, changing its shape and hiding the balanced and well-made timber structure. The photograph below shows it re-erected as it was originally designed. One interesting feature is that the first-floor infill was consistently of wattle and daub, but the ground-floor was of brick; clearly a distinction was made for aesthetic reasons, or perhaps because brick was regarded as more effective or structurally sounder. It is also more appropriate that the heavier material should be in the lower part. The interior is illustrated on page 60, the chimney on page 49.

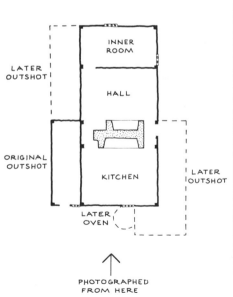

GROUND PLAN

NORTH ELEVATION

LONGITUDINAL SECTION

C A B C

NORTH ELEVATION

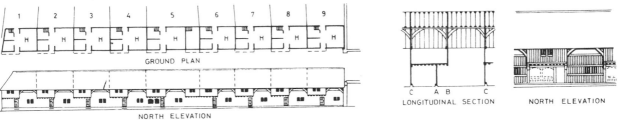

Behind this sequence of varied façades at Battle in Sussex is concealed a terrace of nine Wealden houses. These were first recognised in 1977 and are of a type of 'diminished' Wealden which has been found recently in other towns. They consist simply of a recessed hall and combined service rooms with solar above in the jettied bay. The drawings by David Martin, who discovered this terrace, indicate how complete, yet at the same time concealed, was this long terrace of twelve medieval houses.

97

neighbours. This can happen in many ways, sometimes by the splitting up of a large house or terrace into a number of separate units which do not correspond in any way to the original balanced layout and design. Many medium to large houses of the fifteenth century, including many isolated farmhouses, were subdivided at a later date into shops, semi-detached cottages, and so on. Often part of one house in a village street became part of another, separately occupied, painted and decorated.

These kinds of alteration make the work of interpretation, and the effort to realise the original character of a building, extremely difficult. The older a building – or perhaps one should say, the core of a building – the less likely is it to be recognised from any external survey. For this reason the listing carried out under the Town and Country Planning Act of 1947 of buildings of 'Architectural or Historic Importance' is, in fact, singularly incomplete and misleading, since the investigators had no right of entry. How incomplete has been demonstrated in recent years when intensive surveys of a limited area, such as a parish or a high street has in some cases revealed as many buildings of architectural and historic interest unrecorded as there had been recorded under the Act – or, if noted, listed for details of much later date and of less significance.

The Town and Country Planning Act of 1947, and the Act of 1968 under which whole areas within villages and towns can be designated as 'conservation areas' may now prevent the worst examples of insensitive redevelopment. What is needed, however, is not the ossification of the past, or of arbitrarily selected areas, but such a genuine appreciation of local traditions that the new is almost instictively related to these traditions. Adaptations and alteration are unavoidable, and such adaptations from the sixteenth to the nineteenth century have often been as ruthless and destructive as anything in the twentieth century; the only difference is that it was several times slower, and there was a little more time to think over what was being done. Today the number of simple houses and farmsteads, which, although recognised as being of some architectural or historic interest, have nevertheless been destroyed within the last thirty years is probably

A typical huddle of houses in Lewes, Sussex, varying in date from the fifteenth to the nineteenth centuries – a slow organic development over a long period of time.

far greater than occurred in any previous hundred years; the only positive gain is that a few – but only a very small proportion of the total – have been carefully restored and preserved as a kind of token reminder that there has been a past. This still leaves the main problem unsolved – how should we deal with the many surviving old buildings? One answer may be the exact opposite to the eighteenth-century practice of refaçading – i.e. to preserve and restore the original

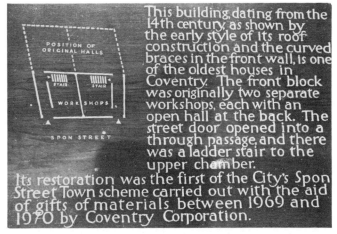

This building dating from the 14th century, as shown by the early style of its roof construction and the curved braces in the front wall, is one of the oldest houses in Coventry. The front block was originally two separate workshops, each with an open hall at the back. The street door opened into a through passage and there was a ladder stair to the upper chamber.

Its restoration was the first of the City's Spon Street Town scheme carried out with the aid of gifts of materials between 1969 and 1970 by Coventry Corporation.

Part of Spon Street, Coventry. After the war a scheme to preserve such early buildings as still survive was adopted. To this street in which a few fifteenth- and sixteenth-century houses remain, it was decided to remove isolated survivals from other parts of the city, to create a kind of museum street. After they have been restored as far as possible to their original form, the buildings will be let commercially. This is one way of dealing with the problem of conservation in an area under pressure for development and redevelopment. The right-hand photograph is of the simple explanatory panel attached to the doorway in the left-hand picture.

façade and reconstruct the rest. In some cases this may be the only solution. But houses, like the parish church, can be a mirror of the growth and changing values of the community. Just as every window, monument, added aisle or chapel of a church is significant of some phase in its history, so, to a limited degree, are the elements of the cottage or the farmhouse, and one does not want to destroy the sense of organic change and development. The problem is, however, more difficult than in the case of the church, since the original fabric is often far more completely concealed or distorted. The exposure of parts of the original building and some later phases in its development is probably the right answer whenever this is practicable. These exposed parts should be sufficient to carry a depth of meaning to those who know enough to be able to interpret their significance. It can then be left to the museums and the buildings selected for total restoration to provide the key to understanding and appreciation.

Part of a comprehensive scheme of restoration and redevelopment at Alcester, Warwickshire. A mixed and run-down group of timber buildings has been combined satisfactorily with a modern scheme for Old People's flats. It won a high award in the Architectural Heritage Year.

Another imaginative treatment, this time in Shrewsbury of a very mixed group of timber buildings near the centre of the town. The photograph is looking from the left-hand side of the plan below.

and tried to meet the challenge in various ways. Leaving aside the purely speculative builders and designers of low-cost housing for industrial workers or farm labourers, they were far more conscious of the landscape and of environmental ties than we have been in the first half of the twentieth century. Unfortunately the requirements of the newly industrialised society led to much 'synthetic' architecture, emanating from the drawing-boards of sophisticated urbanised designers, and it is rare to find a Victorian building with the natural-seeming proportions and homogeneity which up to the eighteenth century had been the rule rather than the exception; but in some areas, such as the Cotswold stone regions, local traditions were kept alive, through the influence of men such as William Morris. Today this area furnishes an example of the failure of the twentieth century to meet the same problem. There is some control of colour and over the use of materials which will harmonise with the local stone: a brownish-grey concrete tile on a roof in that district is better

This leads to the related, but very different question – the decline or debasement of past traditions and the self-conscious revival of traditions already dead. Responsible Victorians were very much concerned with this problem

The County Library at Midhurst (Sussex). A conversion of three very small and derelict cottages by the simple expedient of gutting them of all dividing walls, partitions and floors, and so creating an effective hall and preserving the external appearance. The structure internally is completely exposed.

Artificial stone with a lining of breeze blocks being used in a development in the Cotswolds. An attempt to creat harmony.

Knaresborough, Yorkshire. Housing development by the local council which won an award from the Civic Trust. The use of the local stone is certainly to be commended, but detailing and window treatment could be regarded as unfortunate.

than a red clay tile which might be perfectly appropriate in parts of East Anglia; but colour and texture of materials is not all. The pitch of the roof and the general proportion of a building are equally – if not more – important. A flatter pitch is considerably cheaper and quite as efficient if concrete tiles are used, but the effect can be devastating. A complete break with tradition might even be preferable.

The decline and debasement of local traditions is only one aspect of the problem; another is the conscious revival of traditions already dead. It started with the Romantic movement

of the latter half of the eighteenth century, with the sentimental and enthusiastic cult of the picturesque and the cottage ornée. This can be seen most completely in the design of such villages as Blaise Hamlet near Bristol, or Edensor near Chatsworth in Derbyshire.

The difficulty is that all these self-conscious efforts took little real account of the landscape or natural environment. They were imposed on the landscape – and not derived from the landscape, from the contours, the climate, or the local materials. The 'chalets' at Blaise Hamlet or at Edensor were related in idea to the 'Swiss Village' at Versailles, but none of them had any relationship to the life or the environment in which they were set.

What started as a kind of aristocratic game became by the end of the nineteenth century a popular cult and hardly any village or town has not its 'mock Tudor' cottages, shops, pubs, and even banks and post offices. Even where these are not the most offensive types of sham, such as boards tacked on plaster or merely painted on plaster, they rarely show any respect for, or understanding of, the genuine local forms of timber-framing or decoration. Thus they introduce an

Blaise Hamlet, near Bristol. A fantasy in 'make-believe traditional' by Nash in 1811, to satisfy the vogue for the picturesque. It has neither relationship to the locality nor to any kind of continuity with the past – an amalgam of evocative architectural references. It is in this period that the seeds were sown which a century later filled every town and village with mock Tudor, mock Gothic, and other creations.

element of confusion which results in the actual devaluation of these traditions, and in this way they can be more subtly destructive of any appreciation of the real thing than the juxtaposition of a frankly modern building, asserting forcefully its place in time. However visually inappropriate or undesirable such a building may be, the mere shock of contrast may sharpen our awareness; whereas the other not only confuses but cheapens.

It is the lapsed traditions in timber-framed building which are mostly subject to this kind of perversion; but there are many areas where the traditional use of local stone has continued right up to the present century, and could justifiably be revived or helped to continue if only the added cost – as compared with mass-produced alien material – could be met in some practicable way such as by subsidy. As the object would be to improve the general environment which we all share, this would not seem to be unreasonable.

Adaptation to a new age? A pair of cottages at the Centre for Alternative Technology at Machynlleth in Wales. The cottage on the left has been fitted with 'solar heating' panels.

An estate lodge dated 1826. Almost every cliché has been used in the design of this 'cottage ornée'. No movement could have done more to destroy genuine vernacular and traditional building than the cult of the picturesque which was inspired by a superficial attraction to the past or to the vernacular, without any understanding of what tradition or vernacular really meant.

Recommended Further Reading

W.H. GODFREY, *Our Building Inheritance* (1946).
  Published just after the war, this brief account of buildings suitably and unsuitably restored is still relevant.

NEVILLE WHITTAKER, *The House and Cottage Handbook*.
  This recent publication by the Civic Trust for the North-East is up to date and particularly relevant to the north of England, though a few illustrations are taken from other parts.

H.M. Stationery Office has published since the war a number of useful and well illustrated guides to restoration, and the design of new buildings:
  New Life for Old Buildings (1971)
  Design in Town and Village (1953)
  Various 'Housing manuals', etc.
  Monuments Threatened or Destroyed, select list, 1956–1962.
  This is a strong indictment of post-war insensitivity to our building heritage.

Gazetteer

For the purposes of this Gazetteer the country has been divided into seven regions – but local patterns of building and basic geology do not fit neatly into these divisions, and there is much overlapping and interpenetration. The maps indicate the main underlying geological divisions. The buildings included are those which in the author's view are sufficiently significant, accessible, and fall within the traditional and vernacular category. Buildings which have been mentioned and illustrated in the first part have the page reference. Museums of the 'Open Air' type concerned primarily with the re-erection of buildings as originally designed are indicated by*. Others, where such buildings have been restored but are incidental to other uses by†. For the times of opening and conditions of admission, which may vary from year to year, the reader is referred to such publications as *The Museums and Galleries of Great Britain and Ireland* (ABC Historic Publications); the *Historic Houses, Castles and Gardens* in the same series; *Britain's Heritage*, published by the Automobile Association; the list published by the Department for the Environment (*Ancient Monuments and Historic Buildings*), and the *National Trust Handbook*. The most comprehensive list of farmsteads and farm museums is in the little guide published by Shire Publications, *Discovering Farm Museums*.

A glance at the maps which follow will give some idea of the relative distribution of vernacular buildings which have been made accessible in one way or another to the public (but where groups of buildings are illustrated, access is not to be assumed). Compared with the South-West and the South-East, it will be seen that the East, the North and Wales are relatively poorly served. This partly reflects the relative wealth of the former areas, partly the amount of early and interesting building which survives in them, and partly the current general trend, particularly in tourism, to the South. It does mean, however, that in some areas where there is most need to develop an interest in what may be lost or might be conserved, there is less to stimulate or awaken interest.

Originally it was intended to include an introduction to each of the Gazetteer regions, but to economise space this has been reduced to occasionally extended comments on some of the buildings included. Page references enable the Gazetteer to serve also as a guide to the illustrations shown and as a substitute for an index.

The South-East Region

1. *Winchester*: Pilgrims' Hall. An early example of hammer beam construction. Page 37.
2. *Bishops Waltham, near Southampton*: kingpost truss from the Palace stables in the care of the D.o.E.
3. *Chalton*: site of Saxon village occupied from the fifth to the ninth century, excavated 1974–7. Page 12.
4. *Butser Down and Queen Elizabeth Country Park*: reconstruction of Iron Age farmstead. Page 11.

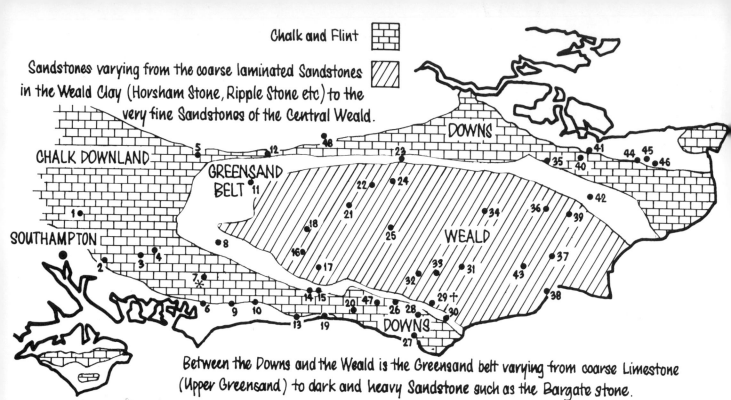

Chalk and Flint

Sandstones varying from the coarse laminated Sandstones in the Weald Clay (Horsham Stone, Ripple Stone etc) to the very fine Sandstones of the Central Weald.

DOWNS

CHALK DOWNLAND

GREENSAND BELT

SOUTHAMPTON

WEALD

DOWNS

Between the Downs and the Weald is the Greensand belt varying from coarse Limestone (Upper Greensand) to dark and heavy Sandstone such as the Bargate stone.

Farnham.

5. *Farnham*: this house (see left) is an example of a form of timber-frame decorative treatment widespread in the West. A good many examples can be found scattered in the South-East, and it is assumed these are the results of contacts or influences from the West. (Cf. Ludlow, page 21.) *Not accessible.*

6. *Chichester*: St Mary's Hospital. This building dates from the last quarter of the thirteenth century. It is one of the earliest examples still surviving of a crownpost and collar purlin roof, which it combines with aisles. This magnificent open hall was originally half as long again. Page 37.

7. *Singleton: The Weald and Downland Open Air Museum. This museum was opened in 1970 and now contains some twenty buildings. The aim is to represent the main types of small-scale traditional buildings in the area. These buildings will be restored to their original form so far as possible. It has provided many of the illustrations used in this book.

8. *Midhurst*: jettied three-storeyed timber-framed town house and County Library. Pages 94 and 100.

9. *Eastergate 4 miles north of Bognor*: two-storeyed granary now used as Parish Room. Page 75.

10. *Arundel*: ruins of the Maison Dieu. Page 47.

Godalming.

11. *Godalming*: a group of timber-framed buildings leading from the High Street to a car park; an example of good restoration and sensible planning.

12. *Guildford*: House Gallery (High Street). Page 24.
    Close by, in the High Street, is the brick-built Abbott's Hospital and the Grammar School nearly opposite.

13. *West Tarring, Worthing*: Thomas à Beckett cottages.

West Tarring.

Late fifteenth-century; part of a terrace of at least four similar houses only two of which now survive. The second house visible on the right is completely concealed by tile hanging and the underpinning of the jetty. These houses are a variant type of 'Wealden' in which the part beyond the dais end of the hall is a cross wing with an end jetty so that the roof line is not continuous. It has a well-preserved oriel window and the remains of a smoke bay behind the chimney at first-floor level. It is now a local museum.

14. *Steyning*: concealed Wealden in the High Street. Page 92. Just opposite there is another Wealden hidden behind a plaster façade and shop front. The High Street contains a large number of examples of such transformations and many of the houses have medieval roof structures of the crown-post and collar purlin type. This and Church Street are described and fully illustrated in *Timber-framed Buildings of Steyning*. See recommended reading.

Bramber.

15. *Bramber*: St Mary's. The corner of a house jettied on two sides; it probably formed part of a fifteenth-century courtyard inn, with a series of small apartments on the first floor and larger communal rooms below. The dormer window is a later addition. The building is a fine example of close studding in which the upright timber posts are set close together with narrow panels of infilling. Close studding can be found over the whole of the South-East of England, particularly in some parts of Sussex, Kent and Suffolk. For another example see page 22.

16. *Shipley*: King's Mill. A smock mill preserved and maintained by the County Authority and demonstrated at fixed times. Page 78.

17. *Henfield*: Woods Mill. A restored watermill forming part of a Field Centre maintained by The Sussex Trust for Nature Conservation.

18. *Horsham*: museum (Causeway House). Page 63. Medieval shop. Page 87.

19. *Shoreham-by-Sea*: the Marlipins, a Norman customs house, now a museum. Page 90. An interesting interior, with the upper floor supported over a central arcade.

20. *West Blatchington, north of Hove*: a windmill built on the roof of a barn. Page 78.

21. *Ifield*: watermill, recently restored by voluntary effort and now a local museum.

22. *Outwood*: a post-mill dating from the seventeenth century and possibly the oldest surviving windmill in the South-East.

23. *Limpsfield*: Detillens; a remarkably transformed Wealden house. Page 93.

24. *Lingfield*: the County Library is housed in a Wealden house in which the hall has been opened up. Some of the details of the restoration – such as the stained glass in the hall windows, are unfortunate. Close by the church is a well-preserved medieval shop front.

25. *West Hoathly*: fourteenth-century Priest's house in the care of the Sussex Archaeological Society and now a small museum. The large open hall has not been cleared of partitions or floors, but the roof structure is exposed.

26. *Lewes*: Bull Lane. Page 98.

In the suburb at Southover is Anne of Cleves' House, now a museum in the care of the Sussex Archaeological Society. The house is similar in form to that at Tarring, but greatly modified and added to. The hall is open to the roof. The collection includes particularly fine ironwork furnishings – from firebacks to taper-holders.

Ifield.

Lewes: Anne of Cleves' House.

27. *Exceat*: group of farm buildings now used as an Interpretation Centre for the Country Park which includes the Seven Sisters stretch of coast.

Exceat.

28. *Alfriston*: Late fourteenth-century Clergy House. The first building to be taken over by the National Trust (1896). The hall is always open but the rest of the house is not accessible. Only one wing is now jettied.

29. †*Michelham Priory*: the complex of buildings includes not only the remains of the ecclesiastical and domestic buildings of the Priory, but also a fine barn, a watermill recently restored, as well as a group of secondary buildings, stables and wagon sheds used for the display of folk-life material.

30. *Polegate*: tower mill, restored to working order largely by voluntary effort.

31. *Burwash*: all the buildings in this photograph are

Burwash.

timber-framed from the fifteenth and sixteenth centuries, concealed by later tile-hanging and underpinning – not untypical of the central Weald.

32. *Uckfield*: Bridge Cottage; a Wealden house threatened with demolition temporarily restored and occupied by the local amenity and history society.

33. *Cross in Hand*: windmill. Page 78.

34. *Goudhurst*: Pattyndenne Manor. A particularly fine Wealden house.

35. *Hollingbourne*: Eyhorne Manor, another Wealden house, with an added kitchen with a particularly well preserved smoke bay.

36. *Smarden*: Another village group from the north-east Weald where weatherboard is used more than tile-hanging but conceals in the same way early timber-framed structures.

Smarden.

37. *Smallhythe*: a continuous jettied house (home of Ellen Terry) in the care of the National Trust – together with adjacent barn.

38. *Winchelsea*: a planned medieval town, now a village with a few houses, some of which are built over massive stone cellars. A fourteenth-century stone-built upper hall courtroom is now a museum.

39. *Great Chart*: Pest house. Page 84.

40. *Ospringe*: Maison Dieu. Timber framing over a ground-floor storey of stone. Well-preserved crown-post roof; in the care of the D.o.E.

41. *Faversham*: Group of jettied houses with gable ends facing on to Abbey Street. Typically close-packed urban buildings with parallel roofs and drainage gutters between. Faversham has three jettied upper halls — the Old Grammar School, the Market Hall, and H.M.S. Hazarde.

Abbey Street contains many early timber buildings behind late façades.

Faversham.

42. *Brook*: A small museum devoted to agriculture and maintained by Wye College. There is a fine barn with oast house adjacent. Pages 73 and 81.

43. *Newenden*: Frogholt. A small end-jettied cottage; restored and accessible. Page 38.

44. *Canterbury*: Shares with York the retention of the best surviving profiles of jettied buildings in a narrow medieval street.

It also has the largest number (7) of surviving medieval inns or pilgrims' hostels to be found in one town.

The John Smith Almshouses (page 85) reflect Dutch influences in the area. *Not accessible*.

45. *Fordwich*: Market Hall with jail built into the arcade. Now a local museum.

Canterbury.

Wickhambreux.

46. *Wickhambreux*: part of a building known as the Old Post Office. An example of squared stone and knapped flint chequer-board walling, with an added gable in early brick and a window, again showing Netherlandish influence. A large number of refugees from the religious wars on the Continent settled in this part of Kent in the late sixteenth century.

47. *Stanmer*: a late eighteenth-century and early nineteenth-century estate village preserving on the village green a

horizontal horse gin and at the manor house a vertical treadwheel for raising water.

48. *Cheam*: 'Whitehall', a late medieval timber-framed house, now a museum.

Recommended Further Reading

R.T. MASON, *Framed Buildings of the Weald*.
  A concise study of timber-framed building in the area.
H.M. and U.E. LACEY, *Timber-Framed Buildings of Steyning*.
  A house-by-house survey of the two main streets of one market town; very clear and well illustrated.
J. HARDING, *Charlwood Houses*.
  A house-to-house survey of the older houses in a single parish.
S. SAUNDERS JACOBS, *West Chiltington in Sussex*.
  A survey of a typical Wealden Parish, in this case mainly based on documentary evidence for the dating and history of individual buildings.
R. NEVILLE, *Old Cottages and Domestic Architecture, South-West Surrey*.
  This book, published nearly a hundred years ago, is full of delightful and accurate sketches of buildings nearly half of which have since been destroyed.
K. GRAVETT, *Timber and Brick Building in Kent*.
  A well illustrated survey.

Manaccan (see page 111).

The three major geological areas indicated on this map are:

1. The Chalk and Flint region to the east

2. Oolitic Limestone and Sandstone

3. The Granite areas of Devon and Cornwall

4. Devonian and Old Red Sandstone

5. Carboniferous Limestone and Sandstone

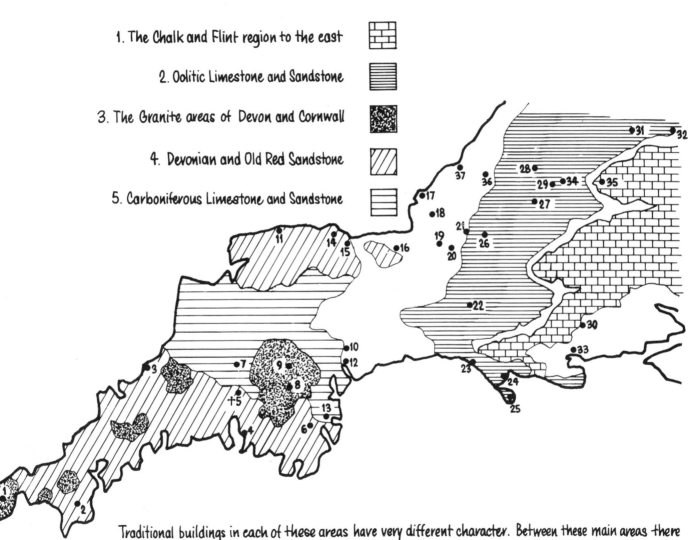

Traditional buildings in each of these areas have very different character. Between these main areas there are a large number of Limestones and Sandstones often giving a special character to relatively small areas ranging in extent from the Limestone to the golden brown stone of the Ham Hill district.
Between the Chalk and Oolitic belt runs the narrow strip of the Greensand strata

The South-West Region

1. *Chysauster*: an excavated iron age village. Page 11.
2. *Manaccan*: A typical group of Cornish Cob. Often an upper storey of cob is laid on a ground storey of stone.
3. *Tintagel*: the Old Post Office (National Trust). Page 59.
4. *Plymouth*: recently restored Merchant's House. Page 46. There is also in Plymouth a fine Elizabethan timber-framed house which serves as a local museum.

Morwellham.

Dartmouth: Butterwalk.

5. †*Morwellham*: Part of a farm complex within the Open Air Museum based on the local mining industry; the museum contains a number of interesting vernacular buildings. The granite posts which support the storey above the open shed are typical of the granite area.
6. *Dartmouth*: the Butterwalk. A group of four merchants' houses of the early seventeenth century. Originally four gables faced into the street. Building over the pavement by an open arcade supported on granite columns is found in other towns in the South-West, such as Totnes. It is characteristic of Breton towns also. Links and similarities at every level of traditional building can be found between those of south Devon and Cornwall and those of Brittany.
7. *Totnes*: a group of warehouses. Page 88.
8. *The Sheldon Centre* near Dunsford, east of Dartmoor. Page 48.
9. *Lettaford*: a hamlet of four houses all of which may originally have been of the longhouse type. One of these has been recently restored by the Landmark Trust, with limited access. Page 20.
10. *Bickleigh Mill farmstead, south of Tiverton*. Page 71.
11. *Lynmouth*: a small local museum is near the middle of the group below which illustrates an effective adaptation of buildings of very different date on a steeply sloping site. One moves farther from the vernacular as one moves up the hill, but the group is held together not so much by the use of local stone or any other feature, but by the surface treatment and colourwash.

Lynmouth.

12. *Exeter*: fourteenth-century Merchant's House. Page 55.

13. *Paignton*: Kirkham House. An example of sensitive restoration of an unpretentious building. There has been no attempt to 'improve' the roughly mortared rubble and red sandstone walls or clutter the interior with irrelevant exhibits or furnishings. (D.o.E.).

14. *Allerford*: packhorse bridge. Page 82. In the care of the D.o.E. Two hundred yards to the west is a watermill restored by voluntary effort and open to the public.

15. *Dunster*: medieval dovecote.

16. *Crowcombe*: upper-floor hall. Page 83.

17. *Woodspring Priory, north of Weston Super Mare*. Page 37.

18. *Axbridge*: 'King John's Hunting Lodge'. This is an unfortunate and anachronistic name to be attached to a fifteenth-century building, now a local museum. A fine example of corner jettying, it makes an interesting comparison with Rowley's House Museum in Shrewsbury. Page 120.

Meare.

19. *Meare*: Fish Warden's House (in the care of the D.o.E.). It is a shell; the first floor and the original fine arch-braced roof (shown in early drawings) have not been restored.

20. *Glastonbury*: St Mary's Almshouses. Page 85. Two other buildings in Glastonbury lie outside the range of this book, but perhaps should be mentioned – the Abbey barn, which has been recently restored and, on a smaller scale, the upper hall of 'The Tribunal' which, like the Fish Warden's House at Meare has a simple arch-braced roof typical of most buildings of medium size and status in the region.

21. *Wells*: Vicars' Close. Page 64.

22. *Stoke-sub-Hamdon Priory* (National Trust). The priory like most of the village, – and many other villages in the neighbourhood – is built entirely of Ham Hill stone. The quarries from which this came are an impressive feature in the flat-topped hill which rises steeply behind the village. As in the Portland Peninsula, some thirty miles to the south, we have an example of an outcrop of particularly fine stone giving a distinctive character to an area with a radius of a few miles.

Axbridge.

23. *Abbotsbury*. One of the great barns of this region, now half roofless and in ruin.

24. *Weymouth, 2 and 3 Trinity Street:* Late sixteenth-century semi-detached stone houses, now a museum. Page 64.

25. *Portland, Peninsula:* This small local museum occupies a house built of the local stone with a projecting porch typical of the area. To the rear and at right-angles is another house also included in the museum, but its gutted interior poses some rather puzzling questions as to plan.

26. *Shepton Mallet*: early seventeenth-century terrace. Page 64.

27. *Bradford-on-Avon*: a remarkably effective treatment of steeply rising ground with flexibility in the individual design of houses, but held together partly by the consistent use of the fine local ashlar stone, and the rhythm of dormer and gable design and pitch. Also, Barton tithe barn and farm buildings.

Portland.

Bradford-on-Avon.

28. *Castle Combe*. Page 19.

29. *Lacock*. Pages 19 and 33.

30. *Wimborne Minster*: view from the garden of the priest's house which serves as a local museum – a good example of the decorative use of squared blocks of local limestone which is quite different from the chequer-board use of these materials in the South-East.

31. *Great Coxwell barn, near Faringdon*. (National Trust). Pages 14 and 31.

32. *Steventon*: a sequence of timber-framed houses. Those illustrated are reconstructions of part of a monastic complex and are now in the care of the National Trust. Part only, including the hall, is accessible.

Steventon.

33. *Poole*: the Town Cellars, a medieval warehouse recently restored and now a museum.

34. *Lackham, three miles south of Chippenham*: small museum located in two re-erected granaries; attached to the agricultural college. Page 75.

35. *Avebury, 5 miles west of Marlborough*: Barn and other buildings housing Wiltshire Folk life museum.

36. *Marshfield, 10 miles east of Bristol*: Castle farm Folk Museum; includes a number of restored early farm buildings.

37. *Blaise Hamlet, Bristol*: Estate village. Page 101.

Recommended Further Reading

G.M. and F.J. CHESHER, *The Cornishman's House*.

An excellent book; there is nothing equivalent for the other counties in this region.

D. PORTMAN, *Exeter Houses 1400–1700*.

Describes in detail a number of houses – some still standing, some demolished – most of them timber-framed, of three or four storeys.

Wimborne Minster.

The Eastern Region

Oolitic Limestone and Sandstone

Greensand belt Sandstone and Limestone

Area without building stone

Chalk and Flint

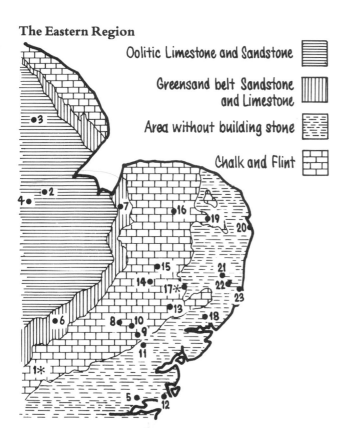

Stamford (ii).

Stamford (i).

Easton on the Hill.

1. *Chalfont St Giles*: Open Air Museum for the Chiltern region, launched two years ago with a fine site and already over a dozen buildings in store saved from destruction.

115

These buildings include a magnificent four-teenth-century aisled barn. A small granary is the first building to be erected, and the Museum is hoping to open to the public in 1979. Page 23.

2. *Stamford*: an old town on the edge of the oolitic belt and largely built of this stone which here is greyish rather than the light golden brown of the Cotswolds. There is also some timber-framing, jettied, but concealed by plaster.

The second photograph (on page 115) illustrates a type of roof construction widely used in Norfolk and areas to the south and west in the eighteenth century. It greatly enlarged the attic space above the eaves.

3. *Lincoln*: this is the only town where two stone-built houses of the Norman period still survive not too drasti-cally altered.

4. *Easton on the Hill*: medieval priest's house near Stamford, built of the local oolitic stone and in the care of the Natural Trust.

5. *Horndon on the Hill*: market or wool hall, a remarkable recent restoration, now used as Parish room and library, but unfortunately the roof is ceiled and only from out-side is it seen as originally built. It is similar in size and

construction to the market hall re-erected at the Weald and Downland Museum. It had been completely con-cealed by conversion to two cottages, with chimneys at each end.

6. *Ashwell (Herts.)*: a small late medieval shop restored and now a local museum. An interesting comparison with that at Lavenham (page 87) as well as that at the Weald and Downland Museum.

Ashwell.

7. *King's Lynn*: Thoresby College. An almshouse (incor-porating an earlier brick-built building of 1500). Un-fortunately the brickwork has at some time been plastered and today has a ragged appearance. The build-ing is of the courtyard plan. East Anglia is pre-eminently an area for the early use of brick. In the east-ern areas the lack of good building stone and a plentiful supply of timber made this one of the great timber-

Horndon on the Hill.

building regions up to the sixteenth century, but after that it began to resort to brick (stimulated by its contact with the brick-building regions of the Netherlands and north Germany) to a greater extent than any other part of Britain.

King's Lynn.

Great Bardfield.

Lavenham.

8. *Thaxted*: a town with a good deal of interesting timber-framed building. The Guild or Market hall with three jettied storeys is one of the finest remaining, much restored and recently cleaned of darkening stain or paint, revealing the attractive grey colour of the oak.

9. *Braintree and Bocking*: Bocking was once a wool town and rather more important than Braintree. The main street is full of timber-framed buildings of many kinds, and one, restored and taken over as the Braintree museum, contains interesting furnishings.

10. *Great Bardfield*: a small two-roomed cottage saved from demolition and restored as a small local museum. One of the few really small cottages typical of a kind once numerous.

11. *Cressing Temple*: two of the finest barns in the country now dated to the thirteenth century. Not open except by request.

12. *Canvey Island*: Dutch Cottage. An example of the Netherlandish influence in this south-eastern area, now a small maritime museum.

13. *Lavenham*: one of the towns richest in timber-framed buildings in East Anglia. The photograph shows the wool- or Guildhall and the house adjacent on the left (all National Trust). There are three carved dragon-posts to be seen, two at the corners of the projecting porch and one at the right-hand corner of the building. It is a fine example of 'close studding' – decorative but not structural. (Page 87).

14. *West Stow*: site of Saxon village where a number of types of Saxon houses have been reconstructed. Page 12.

15. *Thetford*: the Ancient House Museum. Restored with plan and structure well displayed.

117

Thetford.

16. *Gressenhall*: Norfolk Rural Life Museum. A farm complex taken over by the Norfolk Museums Service and run as a demonstration farm. Page 71.

17. *Stowmarket*: Museum of East Anglian Life Open Air Museum with the aim of reconstructing, in particular, farms and farm groupings typical of the region. At present, apart from a large collection of farm implements and equipment of various kinds, there is a barn, a smithy and two con-

siderable buildings, one of which is a watermill complex, with granary, store and miller's house, the other a fourteenth-century aisled hall. Page 35.

18. *Woodbridge*: one of the only two surviving tide mills restored and in working order. Page 77.

19. *Norwich*: Elm Hill. An old street with a large number of buildings traditional to the area. It has been given

Norwich.

particular protection with grants towards restoration. It can be compared with Abbey Street, Faversham, page 108, where most of the houses have received substantial grants from the Historic Buildings Council, and with Spon Street, Coventry, page 99.

20. *Great Yarmouth*: the medieval town which was built on a narrow peninsula was unique. It consisted of well over a hundred narrow streets or 'rows'. After devastation in the war it was further destroyed by redevelopment. Hardly one row now survives intact. Two fairly typical houses have been restored and are in the care of the Department of the Environment as museums and filled with early engravings and photographs which convey some idea of what has been lost. A great many of the buildings seem to have been of brick, a certain amount of which was imported quite early in the Middle Ages as ballast for ships returning from the Netherlands. Not until the fifteenth century were bricks made locally.

Stowmarket.

Peasenhall.

21. *Laxfield*: a jettied upper hall, probably originally a Guild or Brotherhood hall, which is now a local museum. Page 22.
22. *Peasenhall*: The New Inn. Built in the fifteenth century, this inn in a derelict condition was acquired and restored by the Landmark Trust. The open hall is accessible and the rest let as short-term holiday accommodation.
23. *Aldeburgh*: Market or Guild hall. Not so large as that at Thaxted but more elaborately decorated than the one at Horndon.

Recommended Further Reading
H. FORRESTER, *The Timber-Framed Houses of Essex*.
   A condensation of the monumental survey of the county by the Royal Commission on Historic Monuments.
B. OLIVER, *Old Houses and Village Buildings in East Anglia*.
   Written at the beginning of the century; well illustrated.
VANESSA PARKER, *The Making of King's Lynn*.
   A study of the buildings in one town from 1100 AD.

The Midlands and the West Country
This region is the most disparate in its geological structure as well as being the meeting ground of all the major distinc-

tions that can be made in the character of traditional buildings, but the need to provide clearly defined maps gives no alternative. Only the wide oolite belt and the limestone and sandstone divisions in the Pennines are indicated. Over the

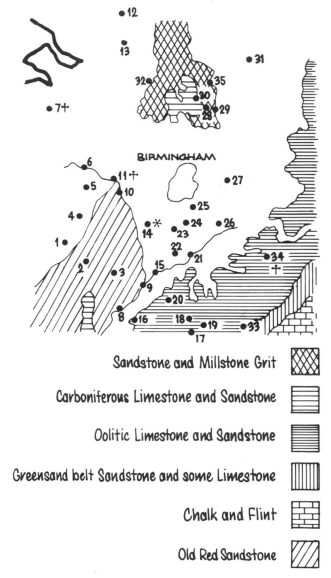

Sandstone and Millstone Grit

Carboniferous Limestone and Sandstone

Oolitic Limestone and Sandstone

Greensand belt Sandstone and some Limestone

Chalk and Flint

Old Red Sandstone

rest of the region outcrops of stone of very different qualities have created a landscape of great variety. Most striking perhaps are the red sandstone areas – dark Old Red Sandstone in the South-West, and the lighter red from different geological periods and loosely defined as New Red Sandstone, which dominates parts of the central area.

1. *Weobley*: a village with a variety of timber-framed buildings including a number with exposed end cruck frames. One or two provide limited access as shops and an inn.

Weobley.

2. *Hereford*: the town museum is in a fine sixteenth-century multi-gabled merchant's house with many pictures of streets now altered beyond recognition. There is also a model of the great market hall which was demolished more than a century ago and must have been one of the grandest and most elaborate buildings of this kind in the country.

3. *Ledbury*: in the High Street is one of the finest timber-framed market halls surviving.

4. *Ludlow*: a town full of timber-framed buildings, mostly of the sixteenth and seventeenth centuries, many with the elaborate decorative style of framing found in the Severn Valley. The Reader's House is open and The Feathers Inn is partly accessible, but both really lie outside the strictly vernacular. Page 21.

Munslow Aston.

5. *Munslow Aston*: the White House Museum; a small rural life museum housed in a range of farm buildings. The house is of particular interest, and of four distinct periods. Reading the photograph from left to right we have: (1) the original cruck-framed open hall (with inserted dormer), (2) close-studded sixteenth-century addition, (3) behind that a stone-built wing, and (4) behind that again a parallel (double pile) Georgian range.

6. *Shrewsbury*: Another town rich in examples of timber-framed buildings characteristic of the area, but also with

Shrewsbury.

as much pseudo period building of the last hundred years. The Rowley's House Museum illustrated is a large merchant's house of the sixteenth century with later additions. It has a remarkably complete ground-floor open arcade. Page 100.

7. †*Erddig 1 mile south of Wrexham*: A group of model farm buildings attached to a great house, relevant in so far as they include the housing for various crafts which would have been associated with such large estates – pit-sawing, carpentry, masons' yard, etc. Very well set up by the National Trust.

8. *Gloucester*: The local history museum is housed in buildings known as Bishop Hooper's Lodging, actually a complex of sixteenth-century timber houses, full of interesting details of construction and decoration.

9. *Tewkesbury*: Fifteenth-century terrace built for shops and small traders, recently restored. Page 63.

10. *Bridgnorth*: detail of Bishop Percy's House, built about 1580, typical of the more elaborate forms of timber-frame decoration in the West, preserved as a museum.

Bridgnorth.

11. †*Ironbridge Gorge Museum*: An Open Air Museum primarily concerned with reconstruction and preservation of a complex of industry and transport associated with the revolution in the smelting of iron which took place here in the eighteenth century. Incidental to this are a few buildings relevant to this book. Page 89.

12. *Bolton*: Typical nineteenth-century terraced industrial cottages. Page 25.

13. *Salford*: in the local museum there is a reconstruction of a nineteenth-century street (façades only) along the lines of the Castle Museum at York.

14. **Avoncroft Museum of Buildings, near Bromsgrove*: this Open Air Museum is not committed to either a strictly regional approach or limited to small-scale buildings of special vernacular interest, but it is the pioneer venture of this kind in England and contains a number of buildings very relevant to this book. It is also concerned with the in situ restoration and care of buildings outside the museum. The illustration is of the first house to be taken down and re-erected on the Museum site, a fifteenth-century house from Bromsgrove. The service end is missing, and in the photograph the cross passage is at the near end, followed by the hall, while the parlour and solar occupy the cross wing at the farther end. The hearth is at the lower end of the hall with the wattle and daub timber-framed canopy

Avoncroft.

intact. The form of the louvre on the ridge of the roof is conjectural. Pages 28, 36, 40, 49 and 75.

15. *Bredon*: tithe barn; one of the great barns of the West Country (National Trust). Pages 34 and 72.

16. *Painswick*: Seventeenth-century house with ashlar front. The lower storey serves as a shop. The whole terrace is

Painswick.

Kelmscott.

18. *Burford*: the main street preserves, with little alien intrusion, diversity held together by a unity of style and material. Page 86.
19. *Witney*: Cogge's Manor Farm, open as a Museum of Farming and Rural Life. Page 74.
20. *Guiting Power, Cotswold Farm Park*: primarily concerned with the breeding and preservation of rare breeds of farm livestock, but centring on a group of farm buildings of interest in themselves. Page 46.
21. *Stratford-upon-Avon*: Two buildings held by the Shakespeare Memorial Trust are particularly relevant – Anne Hathaway's cottage at Shottery and Mary Arden's House at

Stratford-upon-Avon.

typical of the fine ashlar work in this limestone part of the Cotswolds: juxtaposition of houses of very different plan and size yet forming a coherent and satisfying frontage typical of the whole oolitic belt from Stamford in the North-East to Swanage in the South. (National Trust.)

17. *Kelmscott*: another village group typical of the area farther to the south. The less tractable stone from the oolitic belt here is used as rubble with little coursing or shaping compared with Painswick. The building in the middle was the smithy. Page 81.

Wilmcote, here illustrated. Stratford town contains possibly the longest succession of continuous jettied building in the country, page 42, also a large number of timber-framed houses including at least one 'Wealden', and the ornately decorated Harvard House, dated 1596 (well-furnished and accessible). There is, however, a great deal that is sham.

22. *Alcester*: prize-winning redevelopment scheme. Page 99.

23. *Sarehole Mill*: brick construction completely restored by Birmingham Museums Service, six miles south of the city centre.

24. *Knowle, near Solihull*: A group of timber-framed buildings imaginatively restored to serve as a public library.

25. *Lea Ford Cottage* (Near Coleshill): Re-erected by the CEGB in the grounds of the Hams Hall Power Station and serves as a Local Studies centre. Page 58.

26. *Coventry*: in addition to the Spon Street conservation scheme (page 99), the medieval Ford's Hospital has been restored in situ.

27. *Donnington-le-Heath*: small manor house restored as a museum by Leicester Museums Service. Page 61.

28. *Winster*: typical limestone/gritstone area village. Market house in care of the National Trust.

Winster.

29. *Bonsall*: another village where limestone and sandstone meet. Pages 18, 24 and 69.

30. *Bakewell*: the Old House, restored and now used as a local museum. A good interior, open roof and furnishings.

31. *Abbeydale Industrial Hamlet, south of Sheffield*: Page 67.

32. *Nether Alderley Old Mill, twelve miles south of Manchester*: possibly the oldest surviving watermill in the country; in full working order and in the care of the National Trust. Fine roof and walls of the local stone.

33. *Long Crendon*: courthouse. A timber-framed jettied first-floor hall of four bays in care of the National Trust, comparable with such others as Laxfield, Suffolk (page 22) and one re-erected at the Weald and Downland Museum (page 9). The Long Crendon upper hall is restored to its original open form. Page 83.

34. †*Stoke Bruerne*: the Waterways Museum; a complex of eighteenth-century buildings associated with the construction of the Grand Junction Canal and preserved in situ.

35. *Edensor*: estate village. Page 101.

Stoke Bruerne.

Recommended Further Reading

R.B. WOOD-JONES, *Traditional Domestic Architecture of the Banbury Region*.

A detailed study of one small area.

STEPHEN CASTLE, *Timber-Framed Buildings in Watford*.

A survey of buildings surviving in one town.

The North

Only the main divisions are shown;
Cumbria is particularly complex.

SLATE

SLATE

ISLE OF MAN

Carboniferous Limestone and Sandstone

Oolitic Limestone mainly

Millstone Grit and Sandstone

Chalk

1. *Rivington*: great barn. Page 32.
2. *Hawkshead*: courthouse. Built of the local slate, a typical upper hall similar to Crowcombe, page 83. In the care of the National Trust.

Hawkshead.

3. *Grasmere*: the Wordsworth Museum complex. Built of Cumbrian slate with some alteration such as a recent chimney, but otherwise typical of the medium-sized houses of the area. The roof of the bee house at the back of the cottage has a ridge of interlocking slates, a technique found from Brittany to Cumbria, but with few surviving examples in England.

Grasmere.

4. *Troutbeck*: Townend House. A large house in the care of the National Trust with period panelling and furnishing. Adjacent to the house is the 'bank barn' illustrated below.

Troutbeck.

5. †*Halifax*: the West Yorkshire Folk Museum at Shibden Hall. At present the museum consists of the fine house, stables, barn and out-buildings.

•6. *East Riddlesden barn*: this barn is part of Riddlesden Hall Estate, two miles east of Keighley, and is really outside a consideration of the vernacular, but it has a fine kingpost roof typical of the North and is in the care of the National Trust. Page 35.

7. *Golcar*: weavers' houses, restored as a local museum. On

Golcar.

both sides of the Pennines in the textile working area of Lancashire and Yorkshire, 'loom' houses of this kind were built during the eighteenth and early nineteenth centuries before the displacement of the hand loom by power looms in factories. The upper floor (in this rather unusual example two upper floors) was given large windows to light the workroom. Built of local stone these houses are somewhat forbidding examples of the dark hard gritstone of the region.

8. †*York*: the Castle Museum. This is an indoor form of buildings museum in which street façades have been re-erected to illustrate the townscape and urban crafts of an earlier period as realistically as possible. The concern is not primarily with the buildings, or their structure or plans. Of these museums the Castle is the largest and most popular. Another is at *Salford*, called The Street, and there is one at *Kirkstall* near Leeds. The illustration below is of part of the Castle Museum at York. On sloping ground outside the museum there has recently been re-erected a stone-built watermill, fully operative and grinding corn for sale. York is a city full of interest from the point of view of this book, but with no buildings truly vernacular which are generally accessible. Page 42.

9. *Kirkstall*: Abbey House Museum, Leeds. Reconstruction of a nineteenth-century street, shop fronts, crafts, etc.

10. *Knaresborough*: prize-winning development. Page 101.

Hutton-le-Hole.

11. *Hutton-le-Hole: Ryedale Folk Museum. This Open Air Museum is in complete contrast to that at Beamish. It occupies only a few acres, has limited itself to the illustration of traditional buildings in one small area of the Yorkshire moors, concentrates on the small scale and vernacular, and has been built up almost entirely by the enthusiasm of its founder and a number of voluntary workers. It has now eight buildings dating from the fourteenth to the eighteenth centuries, and is working on others. Pages 8, 52, 57, 58 and 79.

12. *Beamish: North of England Open Air Museum. This is one of the success stories of the last decade. Like the early Scandinavian museums it grew out of the need to place

York.

Beamish.

artefacts from the past in a realistic setting, which means appropriate buildings. From the beginning it has been more concerned with the machinery and industrial history of the region than with early traditional buildings. It has, however, some farm buildings and some workers' cottages, and has plans for a large-scale urban complex. Page 65.

13. *Blanchland*: an estate village built partly on a monastic site and using some of the monastic buildings. An example of good planning, mostly within an established local tradition, but with regrettable details such as the ogee window and door heads, and the imitation late Gothic crenellated tower and well-house door head.

Blanchland.

14. **Cregneash*: Manx Village Folk Museum. This small open air museum was the first to be formed in the British Isles. It was therefore a pioneer effort, but is less well known than its more recent successors. Its aims are limited to the illustration of the small traditional buildings of the Isle of Man. These traditions are, in fact, much more closely linked to those of Ireland than to anything in the West of England, Wales or Scotland.

Cregneash.

15. *Tadcaster*: The Ark, a restored timber-framed house serving as a museum.

Recommended Further Reading

J. WALTON, *Homesteads of the Yorkshire Dales*.

R.W. BRUNSKILL, *Vernacular Architecture of the Lake Counties*. This is the first of a series planned eventually to cover the whole country; clear and concise, designed to go with the author's *Handbook to Vernacular Architecture*.

R.H. HAYES and J.G. RUTTER, *Cruck-Framed Buildings in Ryedale and Eskdale*. A detailed study of traditional buildings in a limited area — the Yorkshire moors.

Wales

Except for the northern and eastern counties where a good deal of timber-framed building exists, Welsh traditional buildings are

Slote quarrying areas

Granite

Old Red Sandstone

Distribution of timber framed houses

Area of large chimney breasts

almost entirely in stone, but there is some evidence that more timber building, particularly in the towns, existed in the past. Even in the North-East, as can be seen from the map, it is mainly confined to the river valleys, especially the upper reaches of the Severn. In timber building there seems to be two basic traditions interacting – the cruck, which may be indigenous, and the box-frame which infiltrated steadily from the East from the later Middle Ages onwards. Brick, strangely enough, appears to have been introduced directly from the Netherlands into Denbigh about the middle of the sixteenth century. Everywhere else stone accounts for most buildings, and particularly in the relatively lowland area of the South-West.

Tenby.

1. *Tenby*: fifteenth-century merchant's house, now a local museum and interpretation centre in the care of the National Trust. An interesting plan; the best and largest room is on the second floor, where the wall has been corbelled out to accommodate a hearth and chimney. The stone is a mixture of several quarries, slate,

limestone and sandstone; the corbelling of the corner to clear the narrow passage illustrates how houses were fitted to a difficult sloping site in a congested urban environment.

2. *Penrhos*: a small isolated two-roomed cottage, restored as a museum at Clunderwen, twelve miles east of Haverfordwest. Page 57.

3. *Criccieth*: the birthplace of David Lloyd George, now a museum. One of a pair of cottages, the extension on the left which is integral with the building was a cobbler's workshop. The walls are a good example of the massive, scarcely hewn boulder stone, diminishing in size upwards like the tiles.

Ty Mawr.

Criccieth.

4. *Plas Mawr*: near Criccieth. A fifteenth-century stone-built open hall with a fine timber roof and spere truss, now in the care of the Department of the Environment. No attempt has been made to restore the windows; the interior is clear of any furnishing, the intention being simply to restore and to display the timber structure most effectively.

5. *Ty Mawr, near Betws-y-coed*: Bishop Morgan's birthplace. A sixteenth-century, solidly-built farmhouse now in the care of the National Trust. The rubble walls of the local stone and the typical small and irregular windows have not been modified but the window

frames are quite different from the mullions and shuttering which would certainly have been their form when the house was built.

6. *Llanrwst*: Tu Hwnt i'r Bont. This building, now in the care of the National Trust, appears to have been built in the fifteenth century as a courthouse and to have been subsequently much altered, particularly the windows and chimneys. It is, however, a fine example of the North Welsh tradition of stone building.

Llanrwst.

7. *Conwy*: Aberconwy. Built about 1500 this is one of the few early timber-framed houses remaining in North-West Wales. It is unusual in plan, being jettied on two sides over a two-storeyed stone base on a difficult sloping site. It is in the care of the National Trust and fitted up as an interpretation centre.

Conwy.

8. *Machynlleth*: the Old Parliament House was built in the fifteenth century, and has been completely but conscientiously rebuilt in the hard, jagged dark slate of the area. Within a couple of miles is the Centre for Alternative Technology, page 102.

9. *Tretower*: one of the large courtyard mansions of Wales, now in the care of the Department of the Environment. Although it lies well outside the scope of this book it should be mentioned, as it does include a number of features which reflect the traditional and vernacular.

10. **St Fagans*: Welsh Folk Museum. This forms a department of the National Museum of Wales. If we forget Cregneash in the Isle of Man, it was the first open air museum in the British Isles. It is concerned quite specifically with Welsh vernacular buildings. All the buildings are furnished; some twenty have been brought to the museum and re-erected, and they represent a good many aspects of Welsh building tradition whether in the use of varied materials, types of plan or structural techniques. Like the Avoncroft

Museum in Worcestershire, it has begun to restore and take under its care buildings in situ. The farmhouse illustrated was built at approximately the same time as the Pendean farmhouse at the Weald and Downland Museum illustrated on page 96. Both are timber-built and very similar in size and bay divisions; but whereas the South-Eastern farmhouse had a highly sophisticated chimney structure, the Welsh farmhouse had begun as an open hall, and not until the seventeenth

St Fagans (i).

St Fagans (ii).

century was a simple reredos and canopy inserted. This is the kind of time-lag we need to allow for in any attempt at dating by analogy.

The single-roomed cottage at the bottom of page 130 with an open sleeping chamber at eaves level (or crogloft), is also at St Fagans. It was built in 1762 and is typical in its simple plan of a great many upland cottages. This one is built of very large untrimmed boulders. Pages 11, 45, 54, 70, 76 and 88.

11. *Llanidloes*: the market hall, now the local museum. In this a close-studded timber-framed structure is combined with solid brick at each end. The close studding might at first sight suggest a building in Suffolk or Kent.

Llanidloes.

Recommended Further Reading

It seems quite wrong that a country with such deeply rooted building traditions should be given only a dozen references in this gazetteer, but there are very few truly vernacular buildings accessible to the public. This, however, is perhaps compensated for by the number of important books available.

Fox and Raglan, *Monmouthshire Houses*.

This intensive study in three volumes was published just after the last war, and has served as a model for close studies of limited areas.

Bevan-Evans, *Farmhouses and Cottages: introduction to the vernacular architecture of Flintshire*.

Iorwerth C. Peate, *The Welsh House*.

Published in 1946, already many of the buildings described have disappeared.

P. Smith, *Houses of the Welsh Countryside*.

A comprehensive work, magnificently produced and illustrated; a particular feature is the large number of distribution maps of varying aspects and categories of vernacular buildings.

J.B. Lowe, *Welsh Industrial Housing 1775–1875*.

A well illustrated survey of late semi traditional, and mostly terraced building.

Scotland

Like Wales, Scotland is a large country with a long history, but in some respects more divorced from the mainstreams of English building. The influences and cultural contacts have been different. In Wales there was penetration from the Norman period onwards in the southern areas, and from the later Middle Ages in the North-East. In Scotland, on the other hand, the Lowlands of the South-East were almost equally divided between contacts from across the border to the South and directly from the Continent – particularly the Netherlands – during the age of rapid transition and rebuilding in the sixteenth and seventeenth centuries. On the other

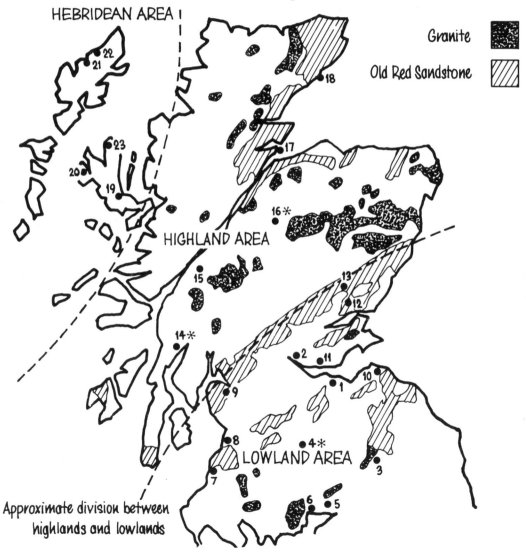

HEBRIDEAN AREA

Granite

Old Red Sandstone

HIGHLAND AREA

LOWLAND AREA

Approximate division between highlands and lowlands

hand, the Highlands remained more isolated and less affected than the equivalent regions of Wales; while the Hebridean areas continued little affected by external influences before the eighteenth century. It seems logical, therefore, to split the Gazetteer for Scotland into three sub-divisions.

The Lowland Area

The Lowlands were colonised by the Anglo-Saxons, Edinburgh being founded as a Royal Borough by the Northumbrian kings. The Border country became a political rather than a cultural division. There is, however, very little traditional or vernacular building which survives, even in the Lowlands, from before the sixteenth century, and by then Continental influences were increasing and had some effect even on vernacular building.

1. *Edinburgh*: Huntly House Museum. One of the few timber-framed buildings surviving in Edinburgh, but little of the box-frame structure above the two stone-built lower storeys is visible. As in Wales, there is a good deal of evidence to suggest that much more timber building existed in the Middle Ages, especially in the towns. Huntly House Museum contains an interesting model of 'The Royal Mile' as it probably was in the sixteenth century, but today the high tenements are entirely stone-built, mostly dating from the eighteenth century, and show much Netherlandish influence in the stepped gables, pantiles, and dormer windows. In the sixteenth century they were, apparently, mainly timber built.

John Knox's House (also situated in The Royal Mile and

Edinburgh: Huntly House Museum.

Edinburgh: John Knox's House.

now a Museum): The stone core was rebuilt in the sixteenth century with various jettied timber additions of different dates. It is possibly the oldest house surviving in Edinburgh. As a museum it is appropriately furnished.

2. *Culross*: a street in this Royal Borough, largely rebuilt from the end of the sixteenth century. In this rebuilding, craftsmen from the Netherlands were employed, strengthening Continental influence. This, and a number of other rebuilt towns, such as Dunkeld, had an impact on style and on detail in contemporary traditional building. Page 10.

Culross (ii).

Culross (i).

The second Culross photograph shows detail of a dormer window in one of the outlying buildings of the Palace. Innovations include not only the form of the dormers and the placing of the attic floor well below the eaves line, but also the use of pantiles as a roofing material, taken up throughout the Lowland area from the seventeenth century onwards.

3. *Jedburgh*: Mary, Queen of Scots' House. This lies well outside any definition of 'vernacular', but it is appropriately furnished and incorporates in one large building both the 'tower' and the 'bastel' type of house as well as a turret staircase. Smaller 'tower' houses can be seen in the grounds of Melrose Abbey (serving as a museum), in the town at Kelso (serving as a

Jedburgh.

centre for the National Trust for Scotland) and also at Culross, the house known as 'The Study'. A large 'tower' house which is virtually a castle is under restoration by the Department of the Environment at Smailholm.

4. *Biggar*: Open Air Museum. An ambitious scheme which will illustrate farmsteads and farm buildings traditional to the Lowland region of Lanarkshire. It should be open in 1979.

5. *Ecclefechan*: Thomas Carlyle's birthplace; a house with archway leading into a yard behind, built by his father and uncle who were masons. The arch plan leading into a court behind is to be found in various Lowland towns.

6. *Dumfries*: Burns' Cottage and Museum. An eighteenth-century town house unadorned and typical, built of semi-ashlar in the local red sandstone. The Bridge Cottage, also a museum, is situated at the end of the old bridge and is a very small stone building with a basement and a loft.

7. *Kirkoswald*: Souter Johnnie's House. An early eighteenth-century cottage with workshop and a rear wing at right-angles, furnished in period. The façade on the street has been whitewashed and only at the back can the quality of the original stonework be appreciated.

8. *Alloway*: Burns' Cottage. This farmstead, now a Burns' Museum, was built by his father about 1750. The domestic quarters have chimneys at both ends; the byre, the store and cross passage lie nearest in the photograph. Below the byre were the pig-sties. The other side of the building fronts the street with main entrance and windows; there is no common entrance to house and byre – it is therefore a modified plan of the earlier traditional 'longhouse'. The building material is mostly cob.

9. *Kilbarchan*: semi-detached weavers' cottages built by a local mason in the eighteenth century and now preserved as a weavers' museum. The plan shows a sensitive understanding of the sloping site; there is no feeling that symmetry was either essential or even desirable. The attic storey is lit by small end gable windows, a tradition earlier than the dormer form spreading from the East.

Kilbarchan.

10. *East Linton*: Preston corn-mill and drying kiln. An interesting group restored by the National Trust; of local sandstone, combined with the warm-coloured pantile which by the eighteenth century became general for the whole of this area. The damp and short summers of the North made drying kilns for oats as essential as a storage shed or granary; nearby is a dovecote of unusual design.

Alloway.

East Linton.

11. *Dunfermline*: Andrew Carnegie's birthplace. This pair of identical semi-detached cottages is now maintained as a museum. The left-hand cottage – Carnegie's birthplace – is furnished in a style appropriate to the late nineteenth century. The building illustrates the development of the double-pile plan in which rooms are set back to back instead of by linear extension (page 67). The width of the cottage facing the street is barely half the depth from front to back. The accommodation is

Dunfermline.

for four rooms (two up and two down) on a frontage of less than twelve feet.

12. *Glamis*: Terrace of twelve cottages. Terrace development in small towns and villages seems to have begun in the Lowlands well before the seventeenth century, although there is nothing to compare with the late medieval terraces south of the Trent. This row of simple two-roomed cottages has recently been restored and serves as a folk museum; the cottage at the far end is furnished in period (eighteenth century).

Glamis.

13. *Kirriemuir*: Barrie's birthplace. A typical example of an eighteenth-century town terrace of three cottages, furnished in a style appropriate to the end of the last century; slightly modified as to windows and interior and with the stonework whitewashed – perhaps to distinguish the three National Trust properties from their neighbours. A communal wash-house in the courtyard at the back is fairly typical.

Recommended Further Reading

For Scotland there is not the general coverage which there is for Wales, but there are the many guides and booklets describing the individual houses open to the public, and of these there are a great many more. One of particular interest is *The Island Blackhouse* by Alexander Fenton, published by the D.o.E. in connection with the recently restored house at Arnol in the Hebrides.

The Highlands

14. *Auchindrain Open Air Museum*: This Museum, six miles south-west of Inveraray, has already been cited (pages 8, 26, 33 and 56.) It consists of the rebuilding of a crofting settlement typical of that South-West area of the Highlands. Although none of the buildings can be earlier than the eighteenth century they range from two houses of 'longhouse' pattern to the more sophisticated and better furnished house of the Registrar (the headman of the hamlet who acted as Agent for the landowner). The forms of

Auchindrain: looking from the byre to the living room in the longhouse.

Auchindrain: exterior of turf-covered roof.

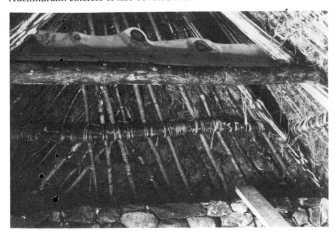

The roof interior.

Auchindrain: box-bed; usually built against partitions in two- and three-roomed cottages.

Auchindrain: the exterior of the longhouse during rethatching with heather over peat-turf underlay.

Cromarty.

construction, however, are remarkably uniform; the building was of local stone with jointed cruck roofs having turf or straw, or heather thatch roof covering, except where corrugated iron had already been substituted before the settlement was abandoned.

15. *Glencoe*: Folk Museum. Three traditional buildings used for museum display and shop.

16. **Kingussie*: West Highland Museum. A small open air museum containing two reconstructions – a longhouse and a horizontal mill. (See page 46.)

17. *Cromarty*: Hugh Miller's Cottage. Cromarty is an ancient town, north of Inverness. In spite of its remoteness it reflects the influence of the Continent and the lowland towns of the South. But whereas in the South the roof behind the crow-stepped gables would most probably have been pantiled, here it is thatched. Hugh Miller commenced work as a mason and became one of the leading geologists of his period – an authority on the Old Red Sandstone which is the dominant building material in this North-Eastern area of Scotland. It is

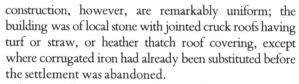

Kingussie: (left) reconstructed longhouse, and (right) the dairy at the end of the longhouse.

usually rather coarse in texture, and this cottage like others may have been plastered and whitewashed from the beginning; but where the local stone could be more carefully cut and jointed, this was done and meant to be seen. The fashion of plastering and whitewashing seems now to be spreading indiscriminately with little regard for the quality of the work being covered, just as it did a century and a half ago in the South.

18. *Dunbeath*: the Caithness Croft. A modified longhouse (independent entry to byre); well restored and furnished; a form of jointed cruck roof with a semi-circular rather than a pointed arch, typical of this extreme North-Eastern area.

The Hebrides

In this area farthest removed from outside influences, early traditions survived almost intact into the present century; but during the last hundred years they have been eroded and transformed at increasing speed. What we have in fact is a telescoping into less than a hundred years changes that farther to the south took three or four centuries. We can see taking place in the Outer Hebrides alterations in plan, construction and the adaptation of buildings to new needs – the kind of changes which were spread elsewhere over several centuries, from open hearth to closed chimney, from the tiniest unglazed windows and openings to sash and, recently, 'picture' windows; from walls five or six feet thick to cavity walls, from turf and heather thatch to tiling (including asbestos).

The following sequence of illustrations attempts to show the way in which traditional forms can be gradually modified until they become so changed that they can no longer be considered 'traditional' – a step-by-step process in which it is impossible to say at what point one has passed from the traditional to the non-traditional.

Note: The first five entries follow the Gazetteer principle of listing buildings open to the public, and are included on the map; the rest are not open and are therefore not numbered, but labelled a, b, c, d, etc., for reference.

19. *Luib*: small Folk Museum and restored cottage.
20. *Glendale*: restored over-shot mill and drying kiln.

Glendale.

21. *Shawbost*: restored horizontal mill. Page 76.

22. *Arnol*: restored 'black house'. A century ago the majority of the farmsteads in this community, situated at the North-West edge of the Hebrides, were long-houses with open hearths. The one illustrated was lived in until 1960 and has been carefully restored by the Department of the Environment, and the interior furnished as it then was. These 'black houses' are, perhaps, among the most perfect examples of adaptation to the environment – to limited resources and harsh climatic

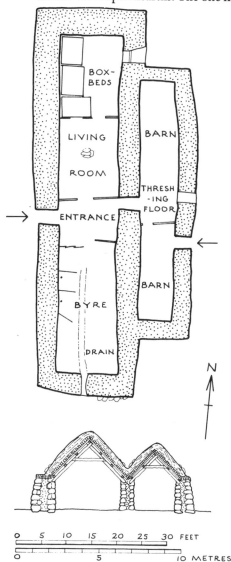

Arnol: Black House (northern end).

Arnol: Black House (southern end).

conditions. The walls consist of a sandwich of peat between outer and inner cases of drystone; the roof structure is of jointed crucks; where timber of any kind was small and hard to come by this necessitated long and narrow buildings. The roof covering is of turf underlay with straw or heather thatch coming down on to and not over the outer casing of stone in order to offer least resistance to westerly gales. The window openings are little more than louvres at eaves level. The houses were the perfect response to the windswept, treeless landscape. They were not small – this one is nearly ninety feet long – and were 'longhouses' in the strictest definition, with a byre directly connected with the living quarter, and common entry. Many were, like this one, of 'double pile' construction in having a barn-and-storage building with parallel roof structure. The cross passage led directly into this rear building, and was still used as a threshing floor. An opening in the barn wall opposite the end of the passage, to provide through draught, was made up with loose, removable stone, when the passage was not being so used.

23. *Kilmuir*: croft, restored as Folk Museum. Here the open hearth has disappeared and instead there are now two hearths, one against each end wall, with chimneys above. The barn, byre and storage are now separate but closely adjacent and situated at the end of the house.

Kilmuir.

The walls are roughly mortared, but otherwise not dissimilar in construction to those of the Arnol black house. These changes, like those which took place in the South during the sixteenth century, are of plan rather than of building techniques or in basic structure. In development sequence, *22* and *23* represent *a* and *b*.

c.

c. Two crofts, the one on the left abandoned, the one on the right slightly larger, inhabited. The structures are similar to those of the Kilmuir Folk Museum but with larger (sash) windows. In both cases they consist of two roughly equal rooms with no loft space.

d.

d. Several changes can be noted. The basic structure is modified – the walls are thinner and plastered and the chimneys and gable ends are built of trimmed stone; the windows are larger and, more significant, the roof space is increased and now used as a loft with two roof lights. The materials of the roof covering have no relationship at all to the locality; only the walls of the derelict storage building at the end preserve some of the elements of the tradition.

e. A stage further, with windows greatly enlarged, the height of the walls increased together with the pitch of the roof. There are now dormer windows, and the house is of the 'two up and two down' plan so typical of

f.

e.

the developments which took place in the sixteenth and seventeenth centuries in the South. The storage building at the end which became an accepted arrangement in the area has been adapted for domestic use. The roof is covered with imported slates.

f. Further modifications; the dormer windows are now a continuation of the wall structure, and the introduction of decorative features such as the cast-iron finial illustrate the adoption of fashions which in the Lowlands date back to the seventeenth century. In the attic a stair and landing between the bedrooms on either side is lit by a roof light.

g. Here can be seen larger windows and improvement in the attic accommodation by the addition of a central dormer.

g.

h. 'Decorative enrichment' has arrived!

i. The introduction of the semi-detached plan – ingenious but recognisably within the stylistic framework of the by now completely metamorphosed original tradition.

j. A further adaptation to terraced planning.

k. Typical townscape on the mainland (Ullapool).

h.

j.

i.

k.

None of the buildings in the photographs can be dated earlier than the beginning of the last century, but the dating sequence is really irrelevant; what we see are a number of buildings all of which in some feature can be related to much earlier traditional building. The process of change has been by step-by-step innovation suggested by or borrowed from the Lowland areas of Scotland during the last two hundred years, just as the developments in the South-East of England from the Norman conquest onwards were repeatedly suggested by, or introduced from the Continent.

To return therefore to the question discussed at the beginning of this book, 'What do we mean by tradition' or 'At what point in a process of continuous change can we say that a new "tradition" has been established?' All we can say, I think, is that truly vernacular building in form, style and plan is rooted in place and the way in which local materials have been exploited by generations of craftsmen, and changes as the community's needs and experience expand. We may consider that some industrial cottages or terraces of the nineteenth century were more traditional in this sense than most Georgian buildings of the eighteenth century, but the line that separates is a thin and wavering one. Urbanisation, mass-production and rapid communications are all inimical to a continuing tradition in any real sense of the word.

This said, something can still be done to conserve these qualities of place and belonging, and to check their erosion and continuing dilution.